POWER MANIFESTING

UNLOCK YOUR FULL POTENTIAL AS A LEADING EDGE CREATOR

NICK BREAU

First Printing, 2020

ISBN: 978-1-64184-272-3 (Paperback)
ISBN: 978-1-64184-273-0 (Ebook)

Nick Breau
www.nickbreau.com

The Free Power Manifesting Bonus Companion Content

My goal in creating Power Manifesting is to guide you in experiencing real transformation. To help facilitate your journey I've created free companion content such as guided meditations, instructional videos, worksheets and other bonus resources. These resources will help magnify the impact and transformation you will experience as you work through the content in this book. I highly recommend you sign up for this free content now.

Visit the following link to get instant access to the Power Manifesting bonus companion content:

http://nickbreau.com/bonus

This book is dedicated to all those in pursuit of living life on the leading edge and pushing the boundaries of what's possible in this physical reality.

Thank you to all those who have supported me and contributed to my growth and expansion over the last four decades. Teachers, coaches, clients, friends, family; and to my collective members, my deepest appreciation for each and every one of you.

TABLE OF CONTENTS

INTRODUCTION

Have you ever accidentally kicked an ant hill?

Did you notice the hundreds, if not thousands, of tiny little ants, scattered, running around in every direction, bumping into each other seemingly uncertain of where to go or what to do?

When I look at The Law of Attraction landscape, I see the exact same thing.

I see Law of Attraction Facebook groups with hundreds of thousands of members. Every third person I meet seems to be a Law of Attraction coach giving different advice on how to manifest anything under the sun. I see hundreds of processes for manifestation involving anything from a cup of water to binaural beats and even an essential oil called Abundance (I wonder how many sniffs it takes to manifest a lottery win?).

With so many options, so many teachers, so many processes (few of which really do work), it's no wonder that for many men and women who throw themselves down the rabbit hole that is The Law of Attraction, most come back out with nothing more than a couple of angel numbers, some good parking spots, a nice string of green lights, some cool synchronicities, and a lot of frustration.

WHY THIS BOOK? WHY NOW?

Because it's time for this landscape to change. It's time to evolve beyond just the basic concepts and the small stuff. It's time for more than just a few people to have the clarity of what's needed to get it right. It's time for you to stop chasing your desires like a dog chasing its tail, and to realize the full potential of who you really are as a creator. It's time for you to get it right once and for all.

As humans, that means stepping into becoming who we truly came here to be – conscious creators of our reality.

> **In this book, you won't find any gimmicks, rituals, or magic tricks that will claim to instantly make all your desires instantly appear. I'm not a genie in a bottle, and, anyway, that's not how The Law of Attraction works. What I will give you is the honest and raw truth about your physical reality, how you create it, and what you really need to do in order to get it right.**

I want to help you earn your co-creational blackbelt.

WHY ME?

What qualifies me to be your Law of Attraction sensei, your Mr. Miagi?

Life experience is the best teacher. Not only have I spent nearly fifteen years on the practice mat and in the ring, I've achieved many of the results that most people are still chasing.

I've manifested a seven-figure sum of money. A dream relationship sharing many synchronicities including similar names (Nick/Anik) and finding out we left our marriages on the same day before we'd ever met. I've manifested a beautiful house on the beach, two amazing kids and a thriving international coaching practice working with clients in over 25 countries.

I've been in the Abraham-Hicks hot seat nearly ten times. I've spoken to large audiences, including groups of doctors and nurses, on the impact of thoughts and emotions on the physical body. I've had clients manifest large sums of money and relationships. I've had clients overcome medical conditions doctors said were incurable. I've trained in over a dozen processes and techniques relating to the mind, the subconscious and human behavior. I've realized the benefits of manifestation in my own life and I've helped others achieve results in their lives.

BUT THIS BOOK ISN'T ABOUT ME. IT'S ABOUT YOU.

In this book, I'm teaching you what worked for me, what worked for my clients, and what I know will, if applied with a little elbow grease, work for you. I'm writing this book to help you understand how powerful you really are. To help you achieve what it is you truly want. To help you bridge the gap between where you are, and where you really want to be.

Whether you know where that is, or not.

No fluff, no BS, I'm going to share the key concepts, the key components, and key exercises that will line you up with your greatest desires, in the hopes of turning you into a Power Manifestor.

Again, life experience is the best teacher. In the chapters that follow you will find what my life experiences have taught me, and it is my hope that they can now serve you.

PROLOGUE: WELCOME TO THE NEW PARADIGM: UNDERSTANDING THE DANCE OF CO-CREATION

If you want to be successful at anything, whether it be martial arts or becoming an award-winning Michelin chef, you need to start with the basics. When it comes to the basics of understanding and applying The Law of Attraction, we're not going to cook an omelet, nor will I have you wax my car.

We're going to start with a proper understanding of what the art of co-creation, and ultimately what real manifestation, looks like.

Just a few months ago, in the -35 degree Celsius frigid Canadian cold mixed with a coastal wind that made it feel colder than the surface of Pluto, I went out to start my car. The car started fine, but what didn't kick in was the heater. For those of you who have the good fortune of living in a warm climate the entire year, what you might not know is that in the dead of winter, a thick layer of ice can accumulate on your windshield. On this morning, that layer of ice was half an inch thick, and without a functional heater to defrost the ice, it took me almost an hour of scraping at the windshield (with some cursing thrown in here and there) so I could head out onto the road.

As I drove down the highway, shivering in what felt like an icebox on wheels, I decided it was time for an upgrade, something new.

A few months later I had set my sights on a vehicle that was newly redesigned for 2019. It was a sexy hybrid, white with a black roof, a well-capable, highly reliable SUV. It was exactly what I wanted. After my first trip to the dealership, they said to come back next month. I did just that, but their delivery got pushed back again, and again, and again.

Finally, the dealer admitted to me that the manufacturer was having production issues due to the lack of availability of batteries needed for the hybrid version of the car, and on top of that, the specific trim I wanted was extra-rare due to the two-tone paint color. He said the best they could do was take a deposit, put in a pre-order and that it would arrive in about six months, if it were to arrive at all.

I went home discouraged. But, since I wasn't in a rush for a new vehicle, I decided to leave it be for the time being and see what else might show up. I let it go.

Three weeks went by, and I kept seeing articles and images about the car pop up on my news feed; on Instagram; on YouTube. I kept appreciating the vehicle knowing that one day it would sit in my driveway. One morning I was randomly inspired to check the online inventory in local dealerships. I checked every dealership within a six-hour radius, and at one of the dealerships, located two hours away, something stood out.

One vehicle matched the exact description of the vehicle I wanted, and it was the same price, same two-tone color, but the model of the vehicle was listed differently. Either they had written the wrong make and model or the description and price on the website were wrong.

I called up the dealership, asked them about the vehicle, and they confirmed that it was the exact vehicle I wanted, and it was available. I arranged to go see the vehicle as soon as I could (two days later).

That afternoon, I also had an inspiration to launch a five-week money group coaching program which I announced the evening before heading to the dealership (more on the relevance of that later).

The following day I made the trip to the dealership and test-drove the car. It was perfect, exactly the vehicle I had set my intent to purchase weeks earlier. The same color, the same trim, it was the exact vehicle I was told would take half a year to show up, and it had presented itself to me in just three weeks. I asked what down payment I needed to make my monthly payments the same as my current vehicle, and the answer was $18,000. I told him I'd think about it over the weekend as I didn't have the cash readily available.

After a weekend of playing with the kids and relaxing in nature, Monday morning came around and it was time to decide. Luckily, it was an easy one. The $18,000 I needed? Can you take a guess at the revenue from the five-week money program I had announced just five or six days earlier? Exactly $18,000.

Within less than a seven-day span not only did I manifest the vehicle, but I also received the inspiration that gave me the exact amount of money needed to purchase it in the way that I wanted. Rather than wait for over 6 months, as I was told at that first dealership, the car was in my driveway within three weeks.

Why am I sharing this story? Because I want you to take note of the process, the unfolding. There was no effort, no struggle, in this manifestation. I didn't spend days or hours in frustration looking for the car. I didn't panic or put any effort into making $18,000 show up. I simply followed a few impulses and ended up with exactly the vehicle I wanted.

Some would say I had a massive horseshoe up my ass. But if you're reading this book, I know that you know perfectly well that luck has nothing to do with it.

In the context of the Law of Attraction, most individuals are focused on very specific outcomes showing up in very specific ways.

How do I make the money show up? How do I make the lover show up? How do I give myself rock hard abs and killer pecs?

The driving force behind manifestation isn't a secret process akin to flipping some proverbial switch that suddenly drops a desire into your reality.

> **The driving force behind deliberate manifestation is co-creation itself. It's the mechanism of synchronicity. That's what provides the magic that allows manifestation.**

It's THE driving force for you, for me, and it equally applies to everyone.

How powerful is this driving force? Not only did it deliver the vehicle and the money, but it timed the arrival of the money perfectly. Had the inspiration for the money program shown up a month earlier, the money would have likely been already spent. Had it shown up later, it could have been too late. It gave me the exact inspiration at the exact time to bring me exactly what I needed to own the exact car I wanted regardless of the production issues and financial aspects that stood in the way.

The first important shift to make, in awareness, is this.

Physical reality, and getting what you want, is not about you working to create something out of nothing. It's about understanding that all of life is a co-creative dance, an unfolding. Most people are not aware of the mechanism of synchronicity or allowing the unfolding to take place, instead thinking they need to take control, figure it out, get there on their own. This is what creates the physical reality experience of effort and struggle, rather than the experience of allowance and ease.

> **Life is a tango taking place between you and nonphysical energy, and physical reality is your dance floor.**

You know what you want, and in this dance, you know where you want it to take you. When dancing with a partner, only one person can take the lead, and nonphysical energy is already doing it. It's been leading you your whole life. But until you let go and learn to rely on it, until you allow it to fully take the lead, it's very difficult for it to lead you. On top of that, it knows exactly where you want to go, and it's trying to guide you there.

But if you're like most people, you're not allowing it.

Your very first step is to take a step back from the effortful process of making something happen, and learn to rely on the mechanism of synchronicity, the magic of the unfolding being handled by nonphysical energy.

This is the one of the keys in learning the art of Power Manifesting.

True power doesn't come from the drive that prioritizes action, effort or hard work. If anything, this removes us from our power. True power comes from a place of being where we learn how to hand over the reins of doing to this dance, which in turn allows magic to unfold in incredible ways.

START DANCING THE DANCE OF CO-CREATION

The more you allow the unfolding of the dance, the more you allow yourself to be led, the more you'll begin to realize there is much more to our physical reality than there appears. You'll begin to truly understand how powerful you really are. You'll begin to realize that life is not, and never was meant to be, a struggle. That it doesn't have to be. That there really is an easier way to do things and a different way to live your life. You'll uncover a whole new paradigm of how you experience your reality.

So, what does life currently look like for most people — for those who are not embracing this dance of co-creation? This is what I call the old paradigm of reality.

Life is hard. With predominant themes of struggle, effort and hard work, you feel stuck and limited. Success is limited by your intelligence, your work ethic, how much you can get done in a day, and how others treat you. You've been taught that you need to keep others pleased and that you're responsible for their happiness. It often takes priority over yours. You need to push and work harder to get what you want. You've been taught, and believe, that hard work pays off. There is much worry and fear of things going wrong. You are confined to the boundaries and rules of how society functions. Things don't always work out, and you often feel stuck and trapped with no way out. The dominant focus of life is to strive for desires, destinations, achievement. Achieving the big things you truly want feels hard, maybe even impossible.

What does it look like when you step onto the dance floor, learn the dance, and begin to experience the new paradigm? What I call living on the edge, being a leading edge creator, and living the new paradigm of reality?

Life simply feels different. Thanks to the mechanism of synchronicity, you've become aware that there's much more to life than meets the eye. You are aware of the nonphysical, that you have an inner being, and of the unconditional love and support that it has for you. Life is filled with magic, ease, and flow. Although fears and worry may creep in on occasion, you understand that things are always working out for you, even when you don't see how. Ease is the norm and you are aware that you are only limited by what you believe is possible. The more fun you have, the more you let in. You understand the value of daydreaming, relaxation and play. Your intuition is strong and the actions you take are always inspired. Rather than spending life striving for achievements, you indulge in the unfolding and understand that the process is the point.

The existence of the new paradigm may sound like a fairy tale. You may not believe in it, or in the stories you'll read in this book. For some, they may sound too good to be true, and it all might sound too easy. But if you've got even an inkling of that deep-down feeling that this rings true, that there is an easier way to experience life, why not take the time to find out? Why not put the teachings you'll find in this book into practice, and see what happens?

What do you have to lose?

My dominant goal for this book is to give you what you really want. Not just what you think you want, but what you really want. A life of freedom, of ease and flow, of effortlessness, of fun. A life filled with clarity, with an abundance of not just money, but of all things. A life where you're so busy enjoying your physical reality you don't care whether the things you're chasing after show up (which is when they typically do, by the way). I want to teach you how to live in the new paradigm because from there, there's no looking back.

From that place, you'll have become a true leading-edge creator.

As you work your way through this book, you'll notice the concepts are split into two parts.

First, I'll be teaching you the dance and how to dance it. What you need to know, what you need to apply, to become that power manifestor and experience the new paradigm of living.

Second, I acknowledge and recognize you likely came here for stuff, to learn how to manifest specific desires, and that's okay. I've spent the greater part of the last decade helping clients all over the world manifest the stuff and achieve what many would call the impossible. I'm going to teach you how to do that, too. We'll explore topics ranging from money and health to relationships. We'll leave no stone unturned.

But for now, I urge you to keep the new paradigm and unlocking the mechanism of synchronicity at the forefront, and a priority, over chasing stuff. Not because those desires aren't important, but because there may be a better way. A better way to experience life. A better way to let those desires in, and realize them. Change your perspective and see the Law of Attraction as a lifestyle rather than a means of achievement: as a better way to live life and a brand-new way to experience your entire reality. Learning to experience it through the nonphysical vantage point, through this dance of co-creation, is a transformation that is satisfying far beyond just manifesting specific things you want.

I love my new car, it's the best vehicle I've ever owned. But what is even more satisfying and thrilling is the story of synchronicity and joy of the unfolding that led me to it. It has boosted my appreciation for the vehicle ten-fold.

Are you ready to learn the dance? In the chapters that follow I will be teaching you the steps to learning this co-creation and the new paradigm, starting with the most important element of that dance, alignment.

CHAPTER KEY CONCEPT SUMMARY

- The driving force behind Power Manifesting is co-creation itself. Harnessing the mechanism of synchronicity is what allows the magic in the unfolding towards your desires.

- The drive that prioritizes effort, action and hard work isn't what fuels manifestation success; if anything, it removes us from our power.

- True power comes from embracing and harnessing the dance of co-creation in ways that allow the nonphysical to take over the reigns of making things happen.

- There are two paradigms of existence. The old paradigm, where most of society currently operates, in which effort and struggle are the norm, and a new paradigm, where ease, flow and abundance are the norm.

- To embrace becoming a Power Manifestor, you want to take the focus off chasing specific desires and turn instead towards living the new paradigm. In living the new paradigm those things you've been chasing will begin to show up effortlessly.

ALIGNMENT

1

UNDERSTANDING ALIGNMENT

What do Coca-Cola, Krispy Kreme, Kentucky Fried Chicken, and McDonald's all have in common (aside from the fact that these foods likely aren't going to improve your waistline)? They're all well- known for having secret recipes.

THE SECRET SAUCE TO LAW OF ATTRACTION SUCCESS

If the Law of Attraction and the art of manifestation had a secret sauce, what would be its key ingredients? Affirmations? Trust? Letting Go? Dancing? Stillness? Backflips?

The first, in order of importance by a long shot, is Alignment. How important is alignment?

> **Alignment is the music that allows you to take part in the dance of co-creation.**

In other words, without alignment, the mechanism of synchronicity cannot play a positive part in your physical reality experience. The infinite intelligence of nonphysical energy is no longer able to lead you in the direction you want. You are finding yourself all alone on the dance floor without your partner to lead you. Without alignment, there is no dance.

Your inner being and nonphysical energy hasn't abandoned you; the co-creative nature of reality hasn't turned its back. You've simply disconnected from it.

Being in alignment is being in your power. Being out of alignment, being disconnected, is like living life as a smartphone without its internet connection. No Email. No GPS. No browser. No Facebook. No Instagram. Not even Snapchat.

> **After air, water, oxygen, clothing, food and shelter, the most important thing in life is alignment and I don't believe that to be an exaggeration.**

When I look back on the unfolding of my physical reality, I can see a clear separation of what I would consider my old life, and my new life.

Nearly a decade ago, life was a struggle. I was averaging fifty hours a week in a cubicle in front of a computer screen. I had only three weeks of vacation every year, with little time to spend with my kids or do what I really wanted to do. Like most people, the money I was making was good, but mostly went into the bottomless pit of payments like my mortgage and other bills. I didn't want to wait until I was sixty to have freedom. I didn't want to wait until my kids were grown up or I was too old to do the things I really wanted to do. I was tired of living my life, like most people, in a state of contentment rather than really enjoying what was possible.

But I saw no way out.

Over time, a feeling deep in my stomach began to develop and grow. It was subtle at first, easy to ignore. But the more I ignored it, the more I pushed it away, the stronger it would bounce back. That feeling was a deep-down sense that life should be easier than this. That there's more to it than this. A feeling that this isn't what life is about, and we're doing it wrong, kept getting stronger.

It may be subtle for most people, but I don't believe I'm the only one who's felt this feeling. In fact, when I ask my audiences during speaking engagements if they've felt that feeling, almost everyone says they have.

That feeling eventually grew from a whisper to a scream and I could no longer ignore it. I had already been studying self-help and playing with energy healing for a few years, but I decided it was time to dig deeper. It was time to get serious about me, about my life, about what I wanted and where I was going, and nothing was going to stop me from getting there, even though I wasn't quite sure where "there" was.

I committed to applying what I had learned over the years. I committed to the principles and practices I had been studying. I stopped simply acquiring head knowledge. I stopped bouncing around from one modality to another looking for the one thing that would work. I realized that if I wanted real change to occur, I needed to do the work, so that's what I did.

My primary focus was to get happy. I understood that beyond the stuff, happy is what we all just really want. It was time to put all the big desires aside, the stuff I believed I needed to have to be happy, and work on getting there without the stuff.

Slowly but surely, I reached for better and better feeling states. As I cleared one source of resistance after another, made one mindset shift after another, circumstances in my reality started to change in very unexpected ways.

Where did I find myself just a few years later? I found myself living in a beautiful home, on the beach, in a small coastal town just two hours away.

I found financial freedom. The company I was working for, for which I played a key role in its early stages, was acquired for over $300 million, giving me the freedom to walk away from my days sitting in a cubicle.

I found myself leaving my marriage, and, nearly a year later, in a new relationship with some incredible synchronicities.

I also found the freedom I wanted to spend more time with my kids. I was now making a living working for myself with my coaching practice, with flexible hours allowing me the freedom to give my kids my full attention when they were with me.

Within a few short years my life was completely transformed in ways I could have never predicted or imagined, in ways my conscious rational mind could have never perceived, none of which would have happened without the mechanism of synchronicity, the magic of co-creation which all started by my working my way into alignment.

That was the first step. Getting into alignment took down a wall that led to everything else.

UNDERSTANDING ALIGNMENT AND VIBRATION

My simplest explanation for alignment is that it's the connection between you and your inner being, or you and the nonphysical, also often referred to as infinite intelligence.

It's where intuition comes from. It's what unlocks the co-creational experience, that mechanism of synchronicity, in your favor. It's what puts you in the receiving mode for the things you want. It allows for a state of flow and feeling of oneness. It transforms your life from predominantly one of struggle, to one of ease. How do you know if you're in alignment? The only true measure is by how you feel.

> **If alignment could be measured like a WiFi connection, it's your emotional state of being that equals your signal strength. The happier, more joyful, and more satisfied you feel, the greater your alignment and the stronger your connection becomes.**

In a nutshell, joy, happiness and feeling good are literally the keys to unlocking your greatest superpower. They are the keys that allow you to start Power Manifesting.

At this point, you might find yourself wondering, Is happiness really all it takes to let it get me everything I want?

Unfortunately, no.

A common misconception in The Law of Attraction community is that all you need to do is get happy and everything you want will fall in your lap. If this were true, then you wouldn't see wealthy people who are unhappy (they do exist, I've met more than a few) or unwealthy people who are plenty happy.

So, what's missing? A second important factor, called vibrational frequency, often simply referred to as vibration.

If you're old enough to remember AM/FM radio, this is the perfect analogy to understand what I mean by vibration.

Each FM radio station has its own station, each station being a radio frequency.

Country music might be playing on 101.5 FM

Hard rock on 104.6 FM

Hip-hop on 107.9 FM

These are individual stations that you can tune into with your radio receiver by adjusting a knob. When turning the knob, the receiver picks up a different frequency and plays the audio coming in from that frequency. All stations are broadcasting all the time, and you simply tune the receiver to receive the frequency of the channel you want to experience.

What most people don't realize is that in physical reality, everything is a vibrational frequency.

A radio receiver tunes into a frequency that is sound (music). Different frequencies give you different audio experiences.

> **The physical body – everyone's – is also a receiver. A translator of frequencies, like a radio. But while a radio receiver translates frequency into sound, the human body translates frequency into a physical reality experience which you experience using all your senses.**

With a radio, adjusting frequency is easy – you turn a dial or a knob. Humans and our physical reality are far more complex, and unfortunately, the human body doesn't have a dial we can twist or turn to adjust the frequency of what we are receiving and experiencing. However, there is a way for us to fine-tune the frequencies that come our way.

Radio receivers adjust the station they tune into using a dial. Human receivers adjust the reality they tune into using their Attraction Point.

Our vibrational dial, which defines the frequency we tune into, and thus the experiences we attract, is what is called your Attraction Point. Your attraction point is defined by what you believe to be true (your perspectives) and what you are observing (where you put your focus).

Everything you experience in your life, from a stubbed toe, to cancer, to a multi-million-dollar lottery win, is a circumstance with which you have become a vibrational match. It is something you have manifested, wanted or unwanted, based on what you have in your attraction point.

Every time you notice a lack of money, you turn your knob and draw more of that experience into your reality. Every time you notice an abundance of money, you draw more of that into your experience. If you believe men can't be trusted, you will attract relationships reflecting that circumstance. If you believe you are unworthy of being hired for a job, you won't manifest it. If you believe you aren't good enough to win a scholarship, it'll be given to someone else.

The above statements are an overly simplified set of examples, because as humans there are many perspectives, including fears at play. We'll dive deeper into taking control of your vibration in the next chapter, but for now understand that what your reality is reflecting to you is always, in one way or another, what you are carrying inside of you. And, that's why in the world of manifestation, happiness alone isn't enough if your goal is the realization of specific desires.

THE CORE FUNDAMENTAL CONCEPTS

We're only into the first chapter, and we've already covered a handful of topics: The mechanism of synchronicity. Alignment. Vibrational Frequency. Your Attraction Point. These four concepts are quite possibly the four most important concepts when it comes to understanding how you create your reality and the Law of Attraction. In order to prevent you from being overwhelmed and make sure you've got crystal clarity around these concepts, let me summarize the definition of each of them, one final time.

Alignment. Alignment is the connection between you and your inner being. The better you feel, the more happiness you embody in any given moment, the more you are aligned. Being in alignment unlocks the mechanism of synchronicity allowing physical reality to favorable ways.

The Mechanism of Synchronicity. The mechanism of synchronicity is what allows for unbelievable unfoldings and magical experiences in your life. It is circumstances lining up in an incredible, coincidental manner and playing out in ways that are favorable to you.

Vibrational Frequency. Radio receivers tune into different stations by adjusting the frequency to match the frequency of the channel you want to hear. Human beings are also receivers of frequency, and by adjusting the frequency, you tune into different physical reality experiences.

Attraction Point. The attraction point for humans is what defines the frequency you tune into and ultimately your physical reality experience. By changing the thoughts you think, you adjust the contents of your attraction point, which then changes your frequency, with the end result of attracting a different physical reality experience.

These four concepts are the pillars that help you understand how the unfolding of your reality occurs. We'll be diving into each of these in more detail, starting with alignment, so that you can master each of them and ultimately shift your way into the new paradigm of reality.

CHAPTER KEY CONCEPT SUMMARY

- Alignment is the level of connectivity between you, and the infinite intelligence of the nonphysical, also known as your inner being.

- Being in alignment unleashes the dance of co-creation, the mechanism of synchronicity, higher intuition. It puts you in the energy of solutions and in the receiving mode.

- After the basic necessities of life, alignment comes next. When in alignment you stand fully in your power and the way you experience life changes in drastically positive ways.

- The key to achieving alignment is feeling good and getting happy. The way you feel is the only true benchmark of your level of alignment.

- Alignment is the first step on the path to conscious manifestation. Without consistent alignment, the art of manifestation is difficult, and we must resort to hard work and effort.

- When it comes to manifestation, both alignment and vibration need to be taken into consideration. Vibration is what dictates physical reality circumstances, including manifestation.

- Vibration is best understood through the analogy of an AM/FM radio. You are also an interpreter of frequency, your reality matching the frequency you are emitting.

- Your frequency tuner is your state of being, also called your attraction point, and the frequency you are emitting is based on perspectives you hold and where you put your focus.

- Your Attraction Point is what defines the frequencies you tune into and ultimately the reality you experience.

2

BECOMING F-IT HAPPY

Working with clients in over twenty-five countries, you meet all kinds of different people having different backgrounds and personalities.

Roughly 18 months ago I received an email from Chris, a young schoolteacher from the Bronx. Chris had read my relationship book, <u>Single No More</u>, and quickly became one of my clients. Although the main focus on our work was in the context of relationships, Chris also shared his passion for working in the entertainment industry and has since manifested some prime-time TV appearances, including a popular game show, *The $100,000 Pyramid*.

One afternoon Chris was busy with some friends when one of them mentioned that the game show had open castings that day. He rushed down to the address of the studio and was one of the last participants allowed into line for the audition. As he waited his turn, he watched YouTube videos on his phone to find out more about the show, which he had never seen.

His audition was a disaster. Having never played the game or watched the show worked against him, and he assumed there was no way he'd get called back.

But he did.

Week after week, he'd get more calls and more interviews. After his sixth call, he received a phone call from the producers who confirmed that he had qualified for the taping and they would send a limo to pick him up and bring him to the studio.

Chris arrived at the studio nervous, but excited. With big money on the line, he didn't want to screw this up. He knew what was at stake and felt the pressure the minute he walked into the studio. Upon his arrival, Chris noticed a good number of contestants were present in the room, more than he had expected. The producers shared that not everyone would make it on the show and that they'd each go through a practice round, to see who would be chosen.

Unfortunately, of the eight participants, Chris was one of the two who didn't make the cut. He went home disappointed, angry and upset. In his mind, he had failed miserably.

That evening, however, Chris was surprised by a phone call from the producers inviting him back for a second taping, to which he agreed. The next morning as he was having breakfast, Chris was visibly stressed. All the anger from yesterday's failure, the nerves, the pressure, and the lack of sleep were clearly getting to him, when his girlfriend gave him a sage piece of advice.

"Don't worry about the money or even winning," she told him. "Just go have fun."

He quickly acknowledged that she was right. That he was making too big of a deal about it all and he decided to just breathe, let it all go, and just go have fun and make the best of it.

And, make the best of it, he did.

The entire day played out in the complete opposite way as it had the day before. Everyone was friendly with him, the energy was light and playful. When he sat down for the practice round, he noticed they were using the same cards as the day prior, so he already knew the answers. He tried to tell the producers and others involved that this was the case, but nobody seemed to care. He aced the practice round, and was selected to be on the show, where he made it all the way to the final round. Chris won $50,000.

This story completely exemplifies the power of alignment. On day one, Chris was in a mental-emotional state that embodied the old paradigm, reflecting back to him a less than ideal unfolding. On day two, Chris relaxed and just decided to enjoy himself and have fun, congruent to the state of alignment which led to his success.

This isn't the only manifestation element to this story. Chris had shared with me that a number of months earlier he had set his intent to manifest two very specific things. To earn a specific amount of money, which he achieved thanks to a nice, unexpected five-figure raise at work, combined with his game show winning; and to have prime-time network exposure to an audience of a million or more. His episode of *The $100,000 Pyramid* was one of the most-watched episodes aired to date, with over 4.5 million viewers.

I love this story for so many reasons: Chris' perseverance; the amazing advice he received from his girlfriend; the fact that the show hit 4.5 million viewers and that Chris could possibly use this on a highlight reel to further his career in the entertainment industry. But what I like the most is how perfectly it exemplifies experiencing reality in both the old and new paradigms.

For some, shifting in and out of alignment can be that easy. For others, it may require a bit more work. In this chapter I'm going to share with you the practical steps you can take, and what you need to know, to work your way into high and consistent levels of alignment.

THE FUNDAMENTALS OF ALIGNMENT

Before we dive into the deep end, here are a few key points of consideration when it comes to understanding alignment.

1. Alignment isn't something that, once achieved, never goes away.

   Alignment is a state of being. It's not a power-up you unlock in a video game that, once you achieve it, is always there. Nobody is always and forever in alignment. The more you practice it, the easier it is to realize, and the more you'll find yourself staying there. But, don't get discouraged for not finding yourself there all the time – this pressure and being hard on yourself for not being in alignment will get in the way and pull you out of it.

2. There's a difference between knowing the concepts and applying the concepts.

   I studied personal growth, including The Law of Attraction, for years before anything ever changed. Why? Because head knowledge alone is just information. If you want a ham sandwich you need to take the ham, the cheese, the spicy mayo, the lettuce, and sourdough bread out of the fridge and make it into what you want. If you want to experience real transformation, you need to take all the information you've collected in your mind, all that head knowledge, and apply it. In your hands, in this book, I'm giving you the entire buffet of what you need to make this work. You've got all the ingredients, but only you have the power to put it all together and eat that sandwich.

3. Alignment is a practice; dedication and consistency are key.

How does someone become the world's top body-builder or achieve their black belt in martial arts? Dedication, practice, and consistency. The more a bodybuilder commits to their eating plan and hitting the gym each day, the greater the results. The same goes for alignment. If you want to master the art of Power Manifesting, consistency and dedication to doing the work are paramount.

Now that we've touched on those very important pre-departure points, let's take off, and help you work your way into alignment.

You don't need to find alignment, alignment finds you.

One of my fondest observations while raising my kids came during toddlerhood. Every single morning, both my son and daughter would always wake up and greet me from their crib with the biggest, ear-to-ear, most loving and happy grin on their faces. As long as they weren't sick with a cold or the flu or in the need of a diaper change, they were happy and excited for their day.

They would wake up happy. They would wake up in alignment.

Our quest for alignment is really a quest in feeling good, in finding happiness. Not just bursts of happiness here and there, but consistent, raw, pure happiness. The same type of happiness you may be able to remember experiencing as a child.

Based on observing my children, and my own memories of being a child, my belief is that happiness is our natural state. And if so, so is alignment.

What does this mean? As in Chris' experience on *The $100,000 Pyramid*, the journey to alignment isn't about seeking it out, it's about letting alignment find you. Chris decided to let it all go, just have fun and be happy, and then everything shifted. It was as simple as that.

So how do we just get happy?

> **Alignment is always there and readily available. Alignment comes when you stop doing the things you do that prevent it.**

LEARN TO CREATE A STRING OF TINY HAPPY MOMENTS

If our quest is to set out to be happy for the rest of time, how would we accomplish this? Do we somehow discover or drop into a state similar to enlightenment that, once achieved, would never go away? Of course not. Should you expect to someday reach a state where happiness is the only thing you ever experience? That isn't possible, either.

But, with the right work, can it become your dominant state? Absolutely. How do we work our way into achieving this? By creating a string of tiny happy moments.

How do we create one entire year of happiness?
By creating twelve consecutive months of being happy.
How about a month of happy?
Four consecutive weeks.
One week of being happy?
Seven consecutive days.
One day of happy?
Twelve waking hours of happiness.
One hour?
Sixty consecutive happy minutes.
One happy minute?
You guessed it, sixty consecutive seconds of being happy.

> **You cannot control how happy you'll be in any given moment tomorrow, next week, or next month. The only moment you have control over is the moment you sit in: right here, right now.**

Those future moments don't exist yet, and they may never exist in the way your mind is perceiving them. Until you are standing in them, they are purely a fictitious creation of the mind.

How do you create a year of happiness? By choosing to be happy right here, right now, in the moment you're in. Then, doing it again, and again. The more you practice choosing happy moments, the better you get at it, and the longer your string of happy moments becomes.

Is it realistic to expect to be happy in every moment for an entire year? Of course not. But what you can do is simply detach and see how many consecutive happy moments you allow yourself to experience. When you drop out, when you break the chain of being happy, that's okay too. Don't be hard on yourself – that's part of the human experience. Start a new chain and see how far you can get.

One of the best ways to practice this exercise is through something I like to call the Be F-it Happy Game. How else can you learn to master the art of consistent happiness?

PLAY THE F-IT HAPPY GAME

The mastery of alignment is an emotional game. It's about learning to achieve and maintain consistent, positive emotional states. But most humans have trained themselves out of the ability to do that, and here's why.

Most humans have given their emotional power away, to circumstances which are outside of their control. Your boss praises a report you just finished. You feel accomplished. Does a neighbor compliment your new landscaping? Your feel proud. The cheese you just bought at the store is moldy. You get frustrated. Does your car get dented in a parking lot? You get angry. Does your son or daughter decide to move to another country? You feel sad.

> **If you're like most people, you aren't controlling your emotional state, your circumstances are.**

Your emotions are likely bouncing around more than a kangaroo on Redbull, and if you want to be able to maintain a consistently positive emotional state congruent to alignment, this needs to stop. You need to take back your inner power over circumstances which you allow to trigger negative emotional swings.

How do you do that?

Most people are trying to control and mold their circumstances to help themselves feel better. They're trying to manipulate their reality, through action and effort, so that it's representative of what they want and what feels best to them. However, life is unpredictable, and the only true constant is change. On top of that, it's not fair for you to put the pressure on other people's shoulders to be or act the way you want them to be, just to keep you happy and pleased. You'll never be able to control circumstances, at least not in this way.

What you need to do is learn to detach. To let go and disconnect from outcomes. To decide that happiness is a priority and to not let any circumstance, no matter how big or small, pull you away from that happy place. This is the be F-it Happy game.

19

A number of years ago, one of my friends, Frank, decided to drop by for a visit and some time on the beach. He showed up with a large case of beer and a frown on his face. His energy felt heavy and I could immediately tell he was in a bad mood.

I asked him about how his day was, and he shared that he spent most of it in anger. "That's unfortunate," I replied. I then asked him how he felt that morning when he woke up.

He reflected for a moment, then said that he had a fantastic morning. He was up early, played some guitar, and made a nice breakfast before heading off to work. So I asked him if he could tell at what point during the day his mood shifted from joy to anger.

Once again, he reflected on my question and suddenly began to develop a smirk. His response? Laundry. Yes, laundry.

He then shared with me that on the way out the door, he peeked in the laundry room, where he noticed a number of baskets of laundry waiting to be folded. Frank expressed with a bit of vulgarity how much he hated folding laundry.

He allowed something as simple as laundry to shift his mood from happy to angry, where he remained the rest of the day. Not only did it shift his emotional state 180 degrees, but he also allowed that emotional state to push him to be an aggressive driver and be extra harsh on his staff at work.

This story might sound funny, but the truth is that virtually everyone, like Frank, allows circumstances to control how they feel. For some, it may be simple things like laundry, or not having enough cream to put in their coffee. For others, it might be a fight with a loved one or the ending of a relationship. Some circumstances will undoubtedly create more challenge than others, with a stronger emotional charge. Dealing with the emotions around a circumstance like grief is obviously going to be much more difficult than having dropped an ice cream cone on the floor.

> **But, in the context of alignment, it's not the circumstances that matter, it's how you internally respond to that circumstance that matters.**

You need to learn how to play the F-it Happy game.

Becoming f-it happy won't happen overnight. It's a muscle you build, a practice you develop that over time, becomes second nature and automatic. The more you practice it, the more you will learn to maintain positive emotional states through your contrasting circumstances, both big and small. I always give this game to my clients in our very first session, and I've had a number of people tell me this game alone changed their life. Playing the game will help you do two very important things - build emotional resilience as well as emotional awareness.

The first step is to have a solid morning practice. This can be a five minute, fifteen-minute, thirty-minute, sixty-minute or longer practice, whatever it takes. It doesn't matter what or how long your morning practice is; the important part is that it helps you feel good.

Morning practice resources including a practice template and meditation audio can be found in the appendix of this book and bonus companion content at http://nickbreau.com/bonus

After completing your morning practice, rank your level of happiness – how good you feel – on a zero-to-ten scale. Zero meaning you're unhappy and miserable (and should probably go back to bed), ten being so happy you're literally irritating to the people around you. You couldn't possibly get any happier. The goal of your morning practice is to reach for and get as close to a ten as possible.

Your next step is to get on with your day, but every once in a while, check in on your happy scale ranking. I tell my clients to set an alarm on their phone and check in every hour or two. Some like to check in during break time and lunch at work. There is no magic formula, other than keeping track of your happy state frequently enough throughout the day to notice when you drop.

Once you notice that you've dropped, your next step is to investigate why. Was it something my boss said? Was it a thought pattern that kicked in? Is it because I still haven't gotten a text from that hot date last night?

The two questions you want to ask yourself are:

1. Did I drop, and what circumstance and/or thought created the wobble that pulled me down?

2. What emotional state is being triggered and pulling me down on that happy scale?

These two questions are going to help you do two things. First, it will help you build emotional resilience.

Let's suppose that today your source of wobble was traffic. This morning you woke up, had a solid morning practice (maybe a workout followed by a healthy smoothie and some motivational music) and got yourself all the way up to an 8 out of 10 on your happy scale. You got in your car to head off to work and on the way there, you got stuck in construction, resulting in unexpected traffic. You get angry, frustrated, and dip from an 8 all the way down to a 4, which you almost immediately recognize.

How are you going to build resilience? Tomorrow, before getting in your car, you're going to remind yourself that yesterday your source of wobble, the circumstance that allowed you to dip from an 8 to a 4, was traffic. Today, you're going to say f-it to traffic because you have no control over it, and just be happy not allowing that same circumstance to cause you to dip.

Every day, you might notice new things that create wobble. And, with each source of wobble, you're going to make a mental note and practice not allowing these sources of wobble to pull you down when they show their face.

Over time, with enough practice, this resilience and the practice of not allowing circumstances to dip your emotional state will become second nature. The subconscious mind is programmed through repetition and with enough reminders, with enough practice of holding that high emotional state, a record will start playing in the back of your mind.

You'll become a master at brushing things off, at maintaining your good feeling place. You'll be one step closer to mastering the art of Power Manifesting.

The second benefit of this exercise is emotional awareness. What you may also notice is that a pattern will develop. You'll notice that the circumstances that create wobble and cause you to dip on the scale always trigger the same emotion(s). For some it might be anger, while for someone else it may be feeling stuck or not good enough. When we have a specific emotion that continues to surface, that continues to be reflected back to us from the circumstances in our physical reality (because it's a vibrational match), I call this a dominant-negative emotion. Learning about the dominant negative emotions we carry is a second crucial step in the quest for high and consistent alignment because these are the gremlins that make high and consistent alignment a challenge.

These gremlins are so important in fact, we'll be dedicating the very next chapter to them. Why? Because dealing with them is the single most impactful thing you can do to achieve highly consistent states of happiness and alignment.

CHAPTER KEY CONCEPT SUMMARY

- Alignment is not something that, once achieved, never goes away. Alignment is a state that in any given moment you are tuning into, or not.

- Alignment is a practice, and dedication to the state of alignment and consistency is key in the art of Power Manifesting.

- Alignment is your natural state. You don't need to find alignment – alignment finds you.

- Circumstances don't matter; it's how you internally respond to circumstances that matters and impacts your emotional state.

- In order to experience long-term happiness, focus on creating an infinite string of tiny happy moments.

- Most people are allowing circumstances to dictate their emotional state. In order to become a Power Manifestor you need to stop allowing circumstances to control your emotions.

- Build emotional resilience and awareness by playing the F-it Happy game.

- Dominant negative emotions are what make high states of alignment a challenge. Dealing with them is the most impactful thing you can do in the search for achieving high and consistent alignment.

3

DEALING WITH DOMINANT NEGATIVE EMOTIONS

Over the years I've attended conferences and given seminars in both Europe and North America on the topics of the Law of Attraction and alignment. When I look at the landscape of people seeking alignment, I see the effort. Lots and lots of effort. What makes something as natural as alignment such hard work?

We've already established that the secret to a high and consistent state of alignment is to identify and stop doing that thing you do which prevents it. Creating a string of tiny, happy moments, establishing your morning practice, and playing the F-it Happy game from the previous chapter has you reaching for alignment and is a step in the right direction.

But why is it that for some people, alignment seems easy and natural, while for others it's nearly impossible? Why is it that some people just need five minutes of morning practice while others may need five hours to get to that happy aligned place?

The answer is simpler than you think.

Let's say you're standing in front of a ladder, and the top of the ladder is alignment. You're also wearing a heavy backpack filled with college textbooks. The thickest, heaviest, most overpriced textbooks you have ever seen. On top of that, your backpack is really, really big. One of those 'I'm a crazy person heading out into the wilderness for a week' backpacks that can fit seven days' worth of hiking and survival gear.

How are most people who reach for alignment climbing to the top of that ladder? First, the morning practice. They start by doing a bunch of push-ups, then maybe some squats. Then, they listen to some music to pump them up. They eat some protein bars, maybe a shake. They tighten that backpack so it's nice and stable and then they start climbing. With all that weight it's a slow, hard climb to the top of that ladder and to alignment. On top of that, due to the weight of the pack, it's a struggle to stay up there for very long and eventually they get weighed back down to the ground and out of alignment again.

> **What's the easier way to climb that ladder? Take off your backpack and put it on the ground. Stop carrying around all the things that make alignment a struggle.**

From that vantage point, you don't need the push-ups or the protein shake. You can just get on and up the ladder quickly and easily while also having an easier time staying there.

So, what's in your backpack that makes your climb to alignment a challenge? What do you need to do in order to drop or empty as much of the backpack as possible, and climb the ladder of alignment with ease?

Your backpack contains your dominant negative emotions.

In the previous chapter, we learned that our reactions to circumstances that occur in real-time impact our emotional state. Unwanted circumstances trigger negative emotions, disconnecting us from our alignment. These emotions are what I call real-time emotions because they are triggered by circumstances that happen to us in the moment, in real time. We use the F-It happy game to learn to effectively deal with these emotions and circumstances, and maintain our alignment.

I now want to introduce you to a second type of emotions, those that you've collected over time and which are commonly referred to as emotional baggage.

Emotional baggage contains emotions that you may have picked up over the course of your life experience, and which may remain unprocessed. I have yet to meet someone who has no emotional baggage. We all have it, but most people aren't aware of it or aware of how to deal with it. One of the analogies I like to use, to explain the unawareness around the emotional baggage we carry, is background noise.

When you walk into your flat or apartment and turn on an air conditioner, it may have a hum or a rattle. After a few minutes, the noise continues but your mind might subconsciously filter it out. It becomes background noise. As humans, we do the exact same thing not only with noise but other things in our reality as well. This includes our emotions.

As a child, let's suppose you grew up with a very judgemental parent who was always making you feel like you were never good enough. Over time, the feeling of not being good enough became so habitual, that you stopped noticing that it was present. The emotion has become a presence you don't realize you're experiencing. Even if you're not noticing it, that emotion is still there.

Why is this important to understand?

> **This is important because it's the number one reason, alongside circumstances, that people struggle with high and consistent alignment. This is the reason that achieving alignment requires so much work for so many people. This is what is filling up the backpack that makes climbing the ladder of alignment difficult.**

When it comes to the emotional baggage that weighs people down and out of alignment, most people turn to a morning practice. They push against the negative emotions in an attempt to overpower them with positive ones. This makes alignment effort and most people fail to realize, there is a much easier path.

YOUR CORK IS MEANT TO FLOAT

If a cork floating in water represents alignment, and these emotions are represented by tiny anchors attached to the cork, what do you believe is the most effective way to have that cork consistently floating at the surface?

Is it to push against the anchors, trying to constantly hold the cork at the surface against their weight? Or is it to remove the anchors, cutting them away so there is no longer any resistance trying to pull the cork down in the first place? The simple answer, of course, is to remove the anchors.

Where do dominant negative emotions fit in under this scenario? These are the heaviest anchors, or the biggest books you're carrying in your backpack when you try to climb the ladder. These are the emotions that, when dealt with, give you the most significant gain.

Let's use 'not good enough' as an example (this is the most common dominant negative emotion I've seen in clients, by the way). Someone who is carrying emotions of 'not good enough' in their emotional baggage will typically do two things. First, they'll seek out circumstances to make them feel good enough to compensate for the negative emotion. Second, if they are seeking out alignment, they will likely use practices such as affirmations and 'positive aspects' lists to increase the feeling of being good enough.

The catch here is that even if they manage to boost the positive state enough to feel dominantly good enough, high enough to compensate for that specific negative emotion, that negative emotion is still underlying and present. Even if you feel better, you've just covered it up and it's still there. The negative emotion is still vibrationally active in your attraction point and you're still energetically pushing against it making the positive emotion hard to maintain. Over time, your muscle will fatigue, and the negative emotion will creep back in, requiring you to go back to the practice in order to boost yourself back up again.

What you want to do, instead, is effectively deal with the emotional baggage. Remove that false perspective and emotion of not being good enough. This allows your cork to float back to the surface and immediately lightens your baggage as well.

> **Once removed, the negative emotion is no longer negatively impacting your vibration and there is no longer a need to boost a feeling of good enough to compensate because good enough automatically becomes your natural state.**

Emotions are a complex topic. We know what they are, but most people don't understand how they work, that they serve a purpose, or where they even come from.

PERCEPTIONS AND PERSPECTIVES

Have you taken the time to consider what shapes someone's emotional baggage? Why is it that one person may struggle from deep-seated emotions of not good enough while someone else may be stuck in dominant states of anger, frustration or sadness?

Life experience would be the most common answer.

Imagine a thirteen-year-old named Sara. Sara was a smart young girl whose grades were always at the top of her class. Straight A's, winning the school science fair, she always worked hard, did her best, and it paid off.

One day however, Sara messed up on a school science test and used the wrong equation. Instead of her usual A, she got an F. Even though she quickly realized her error, it was too late. After receiving the graded copy of her test, she brought it home to be signed by one of her parents.

Unfortunately, Sara came home that evening and her mom was working late. She had to share the test result with her highly judgmental and critical father, who was always very hard to please and often in a bad mood. His response? "How could you let this happen? You should know better than this. Why didn't you study harder? This is unacceptable – go spend the rest of your night in your room".

What went through Sara's mind?

"Wow, I tried as hard as I could, and it still wasn't good enough. No matter how hard I try, I just can't please my dad. I'm just not good enough."

Sara, whether she realized it or not, just anchored in a new perspective (or reinforced one she may have already been practicing), of not being good enough.

These stories are common. We've all experienced circumstances, some more traumatic than others, that fuel these negative emotions.

Was the fact that Sara's father was displeased a true indication that Sara was indeed not got enough? Was the fact that Sara failed a test an indication of not good enough? Was the fact that her dad punished her and sent her to her room, an indication of not being good enough? Of course not.

The more the perspective is practiced, the more reality is reflecting it back to her, reinforcing the perspective (a current reality loop as earlier discussed).

Yet, Sara took on that belief, internalized the emotion into her emotional baggage pulling against her natural state of alignment. She was practicing the vibrational frequency of not being good enough as it also sat in her Attraction Point. Over time, if she continues to practice this perspective of I AM not good enough, reality will begin to reflect it back to her – through her grades, her relationships, the way other people like friends or a boss treat her.

Although this story is fictional, I see this and other scenarios like it time and time again. Especially around the perspective of not good enough. Some people are aware they carry these perspectives, but most aren't. Remember, the Law of Attraction is a law, like gravity, defining the reality you create regardless of your awareness of it.

In Sara's case, how could this have been avoided?

First, recognize that what is anchoring this emotion, is a perspective. That perspective being "I am not good enough," which was formed by her father's reaction. She showed him the test, he reacted negatively, she noticed he was displeased and blamed herself, taking on the perspective of not being good enough, at which point, the emotion took hold.

> **Behind every emotion lies a perspective anchoring it in place. The belief or perspective comes first, then the emotion comes second. Your emotion is a literal indicator of a perspective you have chosen.**

As human beings, we go about our lives experiencing various circumstances. When a circumstance occurs, we analyze it and give it meaning. What does this circumstance mean about me or the world around me? All day every day we are analyzing and interpreting, analyzing and interpreting.

We experience a circumstance, we interpret that circumstance and give it meaning, we internalize that meaning which shapes our emotional state and the feelings we carry.

What does that look like in Sara's case?

1. Sara fails a test, shows her dad who has a negative reaction. (circumstance)

2. Dad was displeased, I can't make him happy (perception)

3. That must mean I'm just not good enough (perspective/ meaning)

4. Emotion of not good enough is now activated, a reflection of the perspective Sara has chosen (emotion).

If you look up perspective in the dictionary, you'll likely find the words "a point of view." Sara's perspective of not being good enough is nothing more than a point of view. It is not a fact. She chose a point of view leading to a negative emotional state.

Could she have chosen a different point of view? "My dad's behavior does not define my good enough-ness." "Just because Dad can't see that I am good enough, doesn't mean it's true." "I failed one test – big deal. He is just overreacting." Absolutely.

These perspectives are no less valid of a choice than the negative perspectives Sara chose.

There is no right or wrong, good or bad perspective. Everyone has the ability to choose the perspectives they desire. My favorite sports team could be the New York Yankees, the Boston Red Sox or the Texas Rangers. I have the prerogative to choose the perspective of which team I like best. I have the freedom to choose that point of view.

Your perspectives aren't limited to just sports teams, or which is the best pizza joint on the block. You can choose any perspective, on any subject. From sports teams to your level of self worth, self-acceptance, and self-love.

> **There is no rule, no standard benchmark or regulation that defines what classifies someone as good enough – who is or isn't worthy, who is or isn't loveable. Negative emotions, when applied to you or anyone else, are just perspectives. They are, simply, a point of view.**

Circumstances have no meaning. You have the power to choose the meaning of circumstance, how it defines you, your state of being, and ultimately your alignment. In other words, you can choose good feeling points of view that are beneficial for fostering states of alignment or you can choose points of view that aren't. Your emotions are simply telling you which of those points of view you choose and the ones you choose always are and will be completely up to you.

If you're like most people, you've been tricked into choosing meanings and false perspectives that have led to the emotional baggage you carry. But worry not – just as Sara chose a non-serving perspective, she can unchoose it. With a new awareness that her father's behavior wasn't an indication of her good enough-ness, she can go back and choose a new perspective, a new meaning resulting in a shift from a negative to a newly formed positive emotion.

After nearly a decade of self-work, I've realized that playing with our negative emotions, as well as the perspectives and meanings behind them, is the most life-changing thing anyone can do. And in the chapters that follow, I'm going to teach you how to do just that.

CHAPTER KEY CONCEPT SUMMARY

- There are two types of emotions — real-time emotions, and negative baggage, or inner child, emotions.

- Real-time emotions are emotions you experience in real time due to circumstances occurring in your present moment.

- Emotional baggage consists of emotions that are unprocessed and which you still carry, resulting from past circumstances.

- Emotions contained in emotional baggage are like anchors that pull us down and out of alignment. Most people are spending their lives seeking desires and circumstances to compensate for their emotional wounds, the emotions contained in their baggage.

- By dealing with the contents in our emotional baggage, we release the anchors and float back up naturally to our state of alignment, rather than needing to push against the emotions that weight us down.

- At the root of all negative emotions is an underlying perspective holding it in place.

- When we experience circumstances, we interpret them and give them meaning through our perceptions. This leads us to forming a perspective which then triggers emotion.

- The negative emotions you carry are simply points of view based on perspectives you've chosen through circumstances you've experienced.

TAKE ACTION – HOW TO ROCK YOUR ALIGNMENT

Now that you fully understand alignment, its importance, and how to get there, your next step towards becoming a Power Manifestor is taking action.

1. Decide to commit.

   Alignment is the absolute most important element of power manifesting and working your way into alignment is the first step. For some it may take a week; for others it may take a month or even longer. If you're ready to discover the life altering power that comes with alignment, choose to commit. With the same level of commitment a martial artist or bodybuilder commits to their practice and regime, make a conscious choice to commit to your alignment

2. Put together a morning practice.

   Remember: the goal of your morning practice is to feel as good as you can on the happy scale. There is no right or wrong practice, no time too short or too long. You can do it in bed, in the shower, in a cave or on the beach.

If you need a morning practice template along with guided meditations and audios specific to your morning practice, check out the morning practice template in the appendix as well as the companion content at http://nickbreau.com/bonus

3. Practice creating a string of tiny happy moments and being F-it Happy.

    How many sequential tiny happy moments can you experience? Play the F-It Happy game. Keep track in a journal or on your phone of how high you get on a zero to ten happy scale and the sources of wobble that present themselves to you. Set your intent to become more resilient to the circumstances that pull you down on the happy scale.

4. Deal with your dominant negative emotions.

    These are the most significant aspects that make achieving alignment effortful and prevent your cork from naturally floating to the surface. We have not yet discussed how to effectively deal with these sources of resistance, and we'll tackle this in the next chapter.

5. Have fun.

    Go at your own pace. Don't put too much pressure on yourself and take things one day at a time.

VIBRATION

AND

FREQUENCY

4

HOW TO ADJUST YOUR VIBRATIONAL TUNER

Now that we've dissected emotions and the underlying framework of how they get created, let's go one step further and start putting this awareness into practice so that you can work your way into a higher state of alignment.

Earlier in this book I shared that there are two types of emotions – real-time emotions that surface as a response to something you are currently experiencing, and emotional baggage, also commonly referred to as inner child emotions. These are old emotional wounds you're still carrying with you from past events.

How do you know the difference between the two? A real-time emotion is easy to identify since it's an emotion you're feeling in your current moment as a response to something occurring in your physical reality.

When you get cut off by a bad driver who makes a wrong turn in traffic; you might get angry. One of your kids tells you they are moving across the ocean; you might get sad. You unexpectedly get a promotion; you feel happy and proud. These are real-time emotions.

The emotions sitting in your emotional baggage, or inner-child emotions, are much more subtle, as they've often become background noise. These are the emotions that sit dominantly in your attraction point and oftentimes we've become unaware of their existence. On occasion I'll have a client tell me they know consciously that they are good enough, but still feel like they are not good enough. When the way you feel in the present moment contradicts what you know rationally, the emotion is likely an inner child or emotional baggage emotion. This is a sign of an unprocessed emotion waiting to be cleared.

Both types of emotions are equally important and rooted in perspectives. We'll look at handling both and we'll start with real-time.

WORKING WITH REAL-TIME EMOTIONS

Picture this.

You're driving down a scenic coastline in your most desired vehicle. Maybe it's a convertible Mustang or a Ferrari. Maybe it's a motorbike or a fancy Mercedes. The top is down, the windows are open, the sky is sunny, and the radio is playing your favorite music. Everything in this moment feels just right.

Suddenly, the music changes. A new DJ comes on the air and they've gone from one end of the spectrum, to the other – this new DJ wouldn't know good music if you dropped it on his or her lap.

So, what do you do? Do you keep listening to it in the hopes that the new DJ somehow gets yanked off the air, or do you simply reach for the receiver and change the channel? If you're like any other sane person, you'll change the channel.

When it comes to real-time emotions you have the ability to do the same thing, it's that simple. Change the channel.

Change the radio station you're hearing by turning a knob or pushing a button.

Change the emotion you're experiencing by changing the perspective you've chosen that fuels it.

The perspective represents the station, and the emotion is the music it is playing.

Any time an emotion you don't want surfaces in a given moment, you can change the emotion you're tuning into, the way you feel, by choosing a better serving perspective. The perspective behind the emotion isn't always obvious. In fact, until you picked up this book you may not have even realized those perspectives existed.

How do we identify the perspective? Simply ask one the following two probing questions:

What must I believe to be true in order to feel this way?

OR

I feel this way because ...

These two questions are going to tell you what station you've tuned into, a.k.a. what perspective you're choosing. Your next job is to choose a better perspective. This is a simple, yet effective technique known as reframing.

As a child did you spend much time watching the old Looney Tunes cartoons with Bugs Bunny? On the occasional episode you'd have a character needing to make a decision. A cartoon devil would pop up on one shoulder and an angel on another. The devil, instigating one perspective, with the angel, another.

In our case, we don't have an angel and a devil. We have an inner being and an inner critic.

> **The inner critic fuels negative perspectives, playing records that reinforce beliefs such as not being good enough, being unworthy, or being a failure. Your inner being, however, fuels the opposite. It comes from a place of pure, positive, unconditionally loving energy, and sees the truth of who you are rather than the false and untrue perspectives being fed by your inner critic.**

In the presence of a negative emotion, the probing question helps you identify the perspective being fed by your inner critic. In order to shift to a positive, more self-serving perspective, ask the following question:

What would my inner being say instead?

Here's a few examples of how it should look:

Circumstance: You experience a breakup. The person you're dating stops messaging you for no reason and you don't hear back from them.
Emotions: You feel abandoned and unworthy.
Inner Critic Thought: People always abandon me because I'm not worthy.
Inner Being Thought: Of course, you are worthy – just because someone else doesn't have integrity or can't see your worth, doesn't mean it's not there. There's a better match for you out there and it's on its way.

Circumstance: You're excited to share some happy news with your best friend and she's not replying to your text. You know she's online and has seen your message, but she doesn't reply.
Emotions: You feel disappointed and let down.
Inner Critic Thought: Who does she think she is! It's so disrespectful. She doesn't care about me. I'm not important to her.
Inner Being Thought: Maybe her own feelings of jealousy from her inner critic are getting in her way, but she really does care for you.

Circumstance: You apply for a job position that you're excited about, and you really want the job, but you receive a rejection letter in the mail.
Emotions: You feel unqualified and not good enough.
Inner Critic Thought: You should have more experience. You didn't work hard enough. You'll never get it right.
Inner Being Thought: You have no idea why they didn't choose you, but maybe the person they chose was best friends with the decision maker. Something better is on the way.

Circumstance: You ask your spouse to clean the kitchen before he leaves because it's his turn to do it and you're late

for an appointment. But upon your arrival you notice that he's played video games and hasn't cleaned anything.
Emotions: You feel unloved and unheard.
Inner Critic Thought: This is absolutely not fair – I feel like a slave. Why do I have to do everything around here? He's so selfish. He must not care about me.
Inner Being Thought: Maybe he had a bad day, felt stressed, and needed to unwind to get back into feeling good. This is in no way a reflection of how much he loves you.

Circumstance: Your daughter just graduated from high school and decided to go to college far away in another country.
Emotions: You're feeling sad and unimportant.
Inner Critic Thought: She's moving so far away; it must mean that I'm not important to her.
Inner Being Thought: She's chasing her dreams and following her inner guidance. Her expanding her wings is in no way a reflection of how she feels about you. The dynamic of your relationship may change, but this change can be positive for both of you.

Like working a new muscle, shifting from the inner critic to inner being perspective will take a bit of practice but over time, it becomes second nature and almost happens instantaneously, without effort. When practicing this reframing technique, there are two skills you'll practice and develop.

First, become aware of the negative emotions as they surface in the first place. Not being aware of emotions as an indicator of perspectives, you may have taught yourself to zone out those emotions, not noticing them when they surface. If you aren't aware of your emotions, you're not going to identify or be able to shift the perspectives behind them. A good practice is to check in with yourself throughout the day and see how you're feeling. If you notice heavy or negative emotions at the surface, use the probing questions to see if you can identify and work through the perspectives.

Second, the reframing. Once you've identified the perspective, it can take a bit of practice to come up with an inner being perspective to counter what the inner critic is saying. Be patient – know that the more you practice, the stronger your reframing muscles will get and the more second-nature it will become. If needed, ask for help from a friend or in our support group in the Power Manifesting e-course (remember, it's free). Your inner being comes from a place of pure positive energy—it always has a positive viewpoint and statement for you to use.

WORKING WITH EMOTIONAL BAGGAGE

Working with deeper emotions contained in your emotional baggage isn't very different than real-time emotions. We often believe that emotional baggage needs to be difficult to clear, will be painful or will take a lot of work. With the right technique, it doesn't need to be the case.

It's not uncommon to encounter men and women who are afraid of their emotions. My belief is that it's a bug in how our subconscious minds work. One of the roles of our subconscious minds, is to keep us safe from danger. Through life experiences, it decides what it believes is safe or what is not. If you crawl under a patio to fetch a ball and you bump into a hornets' nest and get stung multiple times, your subconscious mind will take note of the experience and trigger fears the next time you contemplate crawling under a patio.

You got hurt, and your subconscious uses fear to help you avoid you getting hurt again.

This subconscious safety mechanism keeps you safe and away from danger. It may even be one of the reasons you're still alive. The flaw, however, is that it doesn't differentiate between physical hurt, and emotional hurt.

If for instance you were madly in love with someone and you suddenly and unexpectedly found out they had been cheating on you, you would likely suffer immense emotional pain. Months later, if you're like most people, that emotional pain likely subsided and now sits in the background as part of your emotional baggage.

In this instance, two things now happen. First, part of you wants a new relationship (because, say, you want to get married and have babies), but now you're afraid of it because you could be cheated on again. This is called split energy and will be further discussed later in this book, as it's a critical aspect in manifesting. Alongside the fear of relationships, there is also a fear of exploring the negative emotion because the subconscious remembers how painful it felt. It wants to keep you away from that pain. However, allowing yourself to feel the pinch, shift the perspective behind it, and release the fear, is what you want to do.

In sum, if you're afraid of your negative emotions from the past, have no fear. I've worked with dozens if not hundreds of clients and I have yet to see someone combust into nothingness by focusing on and dealing with emotions.

Now, on to dealing with your emotional baggage.

In mid fall of 2018, Anik and I headed off to Europe for a month to run some seminars and celebrate life with some of my team members who live there. We were visiting climates ranging from Denmark's, which was averaging in the low teens (Celsius), to Mallorca's, in the middle of the Mediterranean, which was averaging near thirty (Celsius). Although weather fluctuations aren't a problem for our Canadian blood, we did need to pack more clothes than usual due to all the climates we would be visiting.

As a guy, I like to pack light. Throwing the bare minimum of what I need in my suitcase usually does the trick, and even though my suitcase was full, I had no problem zipping it up.

Anik, on the other hand, like most women, likes to come prepared. I won't share with you the overweight baggage fee we were forced to pay at the airport but, needless to say, it felt as though it was high enough to feed the entire population of a small country for a year.

So, in what way does physical baggage relate to emotional baggage?

First, understand that different people carry different amounts of baggage. The older you are, the longer you've gone without cleaning your baggage out, the more it likely weighs. But that's okay because no matter how much baggage you have, or how long it's been there, it can still all be cleared.

Second, our emotional baggage is layered. If you're an organized packer, you might put your pants at the bottom of your luggage, followed by shorts, then shirts finishing with socks and underwear on top. Our emotional baggage is also layered. For example, if you suffer from depression, you might have sadness at the surface, followed by anger underneath that, followed by hopelessness underneath that, followed by a fear such as "It's not safe to let that sadness go because if I do I let someone who hurt me as a child off the hook."

When it comes to understanding emotional baggage and how to clear it, being aware of this layering is EXTREMELY important. Here's why.

Above, I used a layering example similar to what I've seen in men and women who suffer from depression. Keeping in mind that no two people have the exact same set of layers, what you should realize is this:

1. Most people are only aware of what's sitting at the surface.

If you unzipped a suitcase you packed over twenty years ago, you've likely forgotten what's in it. After opening the cover, you can see what's at the surface, but you have no idea what's sitting under the socks and briefs you can see at the top. After removing those, you might expose some shirts, but until you look at what's under the shirts, you don't know what's there, either.

In the case of emotions, it's the same thing. You may be diagnosed with depression and have sadness and anger sitting at the surface which you feel most of your day. But what you may not realize, is under those emotions, a few other deeper layers exist outside of your conscious awareness.

2. In order to release the surface level emotions, you often need to dig deeper.

As you dig deeper through the layers, you'll eventually get to the bottom. In my depression example there were only four or five layers, though with some people there can be a whole lot more (I've seen some with close to twenty). Notice how at the bottom of the layers was the belief that it isn't safe to let the sadness go? It's typically the bottom layer, hidden at the bottom of your baggage, that holds everything in place. By finding this bottom layer, and removing it, the whole tower will fall just like pulling the right block out of a Jenga game (assuming you want to collapse the tower).

In my example, that bottom layer was a belief that "It's not safe to let the sadness go" which explains why no matter how much you work on clearing the sadness, it never really goes away with that fear in place.

3. Everything is clearable.

Often times I've heard the statement "This feels impossible to clear" or "I've had this all my life; it feels like it's part of me." My belief is that nothing, no matter how long it's been kicking around, is impossible to clear. Nobody was born with the perspectives that induce these negative emotions. They were all picked up at some point along your life journey, and anything you pick up, you can let go. If you are ready and willing and open to exploring your layers and working through the perspectives, you can let them go.

I've personally spent over a decade studying tools and techniques for dealing with negative emotions and false beliefs that hold people back. In the next chapter, I'm going to share with you a very effective process for working through and shifting the layers of negative emotional baggage.

CHAPTER KEY CONCEPT SUMMARY

- We are often unaware of the negative emotional baggage we carry. Similar to background noise, we carry certain negative emotions so long that we stop noticing their presence.

- When experiencing a negative emotion in real time, you can shift yourself to a positive emotion by simply changing to a different channel. Do this by identifying and shifting the perspective behind the emotion. This is known as reframing.

- Negative emotions are fueled by perspectives chosen by the inner critic. Use the probing questions such as "I feel this way because" to identify the perspective, then choose a more serving perspective by asking what your inner being would choose instead.

- There is no reason to fear negative emotions. The subconscious mind is trying to help you avoid the painful feelings of negative emotions. It doesn't understand the importance of processing and releasing them.

- Everyone has collected a different set of emotional baggage. The emotions we carry are layered in the same way we would layer clothing in a suitcase.

- We are typically only aware of the emotions sitting at the surface of our emotional baggage. In order to release what's at the surface, we often need to dig deeper into the lower layers.

- There is no emotion that cannot be cleared. If an emotion is difficult to release it simply means there is an underlying emotion or perspective that has not been identified and reframed.

5

ADVANCED VIBRATIONAL TUNING

Almost every morning over the course of the summer, as soon as my kids finish breakfast, they ask me the exact same question.

"Dad, can we go to the escape room today?"

My kids love escape rooms. We took my son and his friends on his birthday and so far we've gone about a half dozen times. I'm not sure if it's the themes such as Harry Potter or Jumanji, the puzzle aspect, or just the idea of being locked in a room needing to escape, but my kids can't get enough.

Being an addict to the rush of solving problems, I'll admit I enjoy them too.

What is an escape room and how does it work?

You and a group of four to eight friends are locked in a puzzle room with a sixty-minute timer and have to find your way out. The unfolding typically starts with a riddle, leading you to a key or a combination that unlocks a cabinet, briefcase, drawer or other item. Upon finding that key, opening the item and retrieving the contents, you'll find another riddle leading to another key, opening another item, revealing yet another key, another riddle leading to another key, etc.

Eventually, with enough skill and a little bit of luck, you'll uncover the final key that unlocks the main door, winning the game before you run out of time. How are escape rooms relevant to clearing your emotional baggage? The process of working through those layers of emotions is a game that unfolds in the exact same way.

> **The surface layer emotions you feel are clues leading to underlying perspectives.**

That underlying perspective may be something you can reframe, or it may lead you to another underlying perspective. Then another. Eventually you'll get to the bottom of the chain and find the one perspective that may be holding it all in place. When you do, use the reframing technique from the previous chapter and release the perspective, then work your way back up to the original starting point and kiss some of that emotional baggage that's been holding you back goodbye.

UNPACKING YOUR EMOTIONAL BAGGAGE

In order to work through each of your layers we're going to use the same probing questions we saw in the previous chapters. These are the prompts that will help you solve the riddle of what's laying underneath.

> **What must I believe to be true in order to feel this way?**
>
> **OR**
>
> **I feel this way because ...**

We're also going to throw in a set of three statements, to deal with layers of fear (usually felt as an anxious feeling) that may also come up as you work through the layers.

> **I'm/It's not safe because ...**
>
> **If I do, what's the worst thing that could happen ...**
>
> **What must I believe to be true to feel unsafe?**

Here's a sample of what this could look like:

Emotion: I'm not good enough. (surface layer, an emotion that I notice I'm feeling)
Question: I feel not good enough because ...
Belief: Because my parents were never satisfied
Emotion: This made me feel like a failure (second layer)
Question: I feel like a failure because ...
Belief: I couldn't keep my parents happy
Emotion: This made me feel unloved (third layer)
Question: <keep going from here>

Eventually, as you continue working through the layers, you'll get to a point where your answers begin repeating themselves, or your answers feel untrue and you can release the emotion.

In the above example, we have the statement "I couldn't keep my parents happy" allowing you to take on the feeling of being unloved. The conscious mind may be able to realize in looking at this statement that of course having unhappy parents is not an indication of them not loving you (I see this frequently in individuals whose parents divorced when they were a child). By identifying this layer and reframing and reminding/understanding that this statement is false, you then loosen up and release the emotion of unloved and can then work your way back up. What next? Reframe and release.

LEARN TO REFRAME AND RELEASE

Once you believe you've gotten to the bottom of the barrel, work your way from the bottom back up to the surface, re-framing each belief from the negative inner critic perspective to the positive inner being one, releasing them one at a time.

Sometimes an emotion can split into two or more perspectives. In the above example, the emotion "I feel like a failure" could be rooted in two perspectives, with "I couldn't keep my parents happy" (which was identified in this example) being the first, and "I'm not a successful lawyer like both my siblings" as a second. As you work back up the layers doing the reframing, check and see if you can still feel the emotion after releasing the perspective. If you can still feel it, there is possibly another perspective holding it in place. When this is the case, ask the probing question again to identify the second perspective and keep going.

Here are two real world examples from client sessions, to help better understand what the process may look like.

Real Life Example 1 - It's not safe to play big

This first example is from a coach in one of my practitioner trainings who was afraid to put themselves out there and promote on social media.

Emotion: Anxious Feeling (starting point – Posting on Facebook about my business makes me feel nervous and anxious).
Question: What must I believe is true to feel unsafe?
Belief: I need to play/stay small in order to be safe.
Question: It's not safe to play big because if I do?
Belief: I'll be rejected.
Question: I feel rejected because?
Belief: I'm not good enough.
Question: I'm not good enough because?
Belief: I'm ugly.
Question: I feel like I'm ugly because?
Her Answer: It's not true, that was a childhood belief and I recognize that's false.

At this point, we've gotten to the bottom and we work our way back up the chain.

Question: Do you still believe you are ugly?
Her Answer: No.
Question: Do you still feel not good enough?
Her Answer: Yes, it's still there.

At this point, she has released one of the roots, but that emotion of not good enough has a second perspective.

Question: I'm not good enough because?
Belief: I'm a failure.
Question: I feel this way because?
Belief: I never finish what I start.

Her Comment: But this isn't true, I've finished lots of things.

I reinforce this by showing her nobody finishes everything they start, and she agrees this is no indication of being a failure. Once again, we keep working back up the layers. The feeling of being a failure is now cleared.

Question: Do you still believe or feel you are not good enough?
Her Answer: No.
Question: Do you still feel rejected?
Her Answer: No.
Question: Do you feel unsafe to play big?
Her Answer: No.
Question: Do you still feel that anxious feeling?
Her Answer: No.

Real Life Example 2 - Angry Feeling

The second example is from a client who had a dominant negative emotion of anger that kept her from steady states of alignment.

Emotion: Angry feeling (starting point).
Question: What must you believe is true to feel angry?
Belief: I wasn't nurtured.
Question: What must you believe to be true to feel you weren't nurtured?
Belief: I feel I wasn't protected.
Question: What must you believe to be true to feel you weren't protected?
Belief: I feel I don't come first.
Question: What must you believe to be true to feel you don't come first?
Belief: Mom didn't love/want me.

Question: What must you believe to be true to feel mom doesn't love you?

Her Answer: As an adult now, I realize it's not true at a conscious level, but it still feels true.

At this point we have found an inner child emotion. I have my client visualize the child who feels this feeling next to her and have her talk to her child (in her mind) to show her that she was wanted and her mom loves her.

Question: Does the feeling of being unloved feel gone?

Her Answer: Yes! It's no longer there.

Now we work our way back up the layers, reframing as we go.

Question: Do you still feel like you don't come first?

Her Answer: No.

Question: Do you still feel like you weren't protected?

Her Answer: No.

Question: Do you still feel like you weren't nurtured?

Her Answer: No.

Question: Do you still feel that angry feeling?

Her Answer: No.

In this example, the surface dominant negative emotion of being angry was being held in place by an old inner child belief (which was a few layers deep, and so outside of her awareness) that she was unwanted by her mother. As an adult, she knew this was no longer true, and once she gained awareness of this false perspective being held by her inner child and let it go, all the layers above it, including the anger, released.

This process of digging through the layers is extremely effective. I've been using it for several years with all my clients. Thanks to my computer science background I have developed a strong analytical mind which makes it easy to identify and clear the layers.

If you're new to this type of work, go easy on yourself. This process almost feels like an art form where the flow is different for every individual because everyone has a different set of layers under the surface. Some layers are more easily uncovered than others. The real-world examples I've used were chosen due to their simplicity. The layers some people hold can be much more complex, but it doesn't mean it's not possible to clear them.

Also, remember that you've been forming perspectives and the emotions that accompany them, for decades. You won't clear all your emotional baggage in one night. Be patient – trust the process and continue to allow yourself to deal with each layer as they come to the surface.

In my experience, when an emotion isn't clearing, it's because of an underlying perspective you aren't realizing is present, or you aren't getting to the bottom layer.

Have you ever watched a movie where the lead character, Indiana Jones, for example, finds themselves stuck in quicksand? The more you move, the quicker you sink, and in order to get out, you need to find someone else to throw you a branch or a vine and pull you out.

When it comes to clearing work, when it's our own stuff, it can be like being stuck in quicksand because we're automatically in the energy of the problem. Having a friend who is familiar with the process, who can lead and ask the questions, can often make a big difference. They can see things that you may not be able to realize from within the problem. A friend can be a valuable ally in your clearing work if they also understand the process. If you want to get serious about clearing and want to go one step further, I also train practitioners who combine this process with another tool called Emotional Freedom Technique (EFT / Tapping). The combination of these two processes is extremely powerful and life-changing for almost everyone who decides to commit to the work.

If you're interested in connecting with one of my team members to learn more about assisting you in working your way out of the quicksand, you can find the contact details in the bonus companion content at http://nickbreau.com/bonus.

CHAPTER KEY CONCEPT SUMMARY

- Emotions are clues that lead to underlying perspectives. Use the probing questions to continue to work down the layers until you identify a perspective that can easily be reframed and released.

- Once a perspective has been reframed and the emotion released, work your way back up the layers you've identified.

- Sometimes an emotion can have two or more underlying perspectives. Work through each of these perspectives.

- Be patient and trust the process. These exercises take practice and can take a bit of time – you won't clear your entire set of negative emotional baggage in just one day.

- When dealing with our own emotional baggage, we are in the energy of the problem and it can be difficult to identify the underlying perspectives. Having a friend work the process with you or getting the help of a trained practitioner will likely expedite the results.

6

HOW TO AUDIT YOUR ATTRACTION POINT

Over the last few years I've done several speaking engagements to audiences of various sizes, at events ranging from spiritual and wellness, to corporate groups such as government agencies and healthcare providers. At the end of my time on stage, it's not uncommon to spend an hour privately fielding questions.

Jack, one of the audience members who waited patiently for a discussion, shared that he was curious about why, no matter how hard he tried, he was falling short in every aspect of his life, from career to relationships. He was smart, good looking, well-composed and he just couldn't understand what he believed was unrelenting bad luck or even a curse.

As Jack told his story and explained how he believed his life was cursed, I noticed him massaging and rubbing his left shoulder and neck. So I asked Jack if he suffered from chronic neck and shoulder issues.

"Oh, that?" he replied. "Just an old hockey injury from over twenty years ago that never went away."

I knew immediately that even though from a physical standpoint, his shoulder pain originated from a sports injury, there was still a vibrational root cause. So I decided to dig, and started asking some probing questions.

I asked Jack what he did for work, and he responded that he worked in sales. I asked him if he had a boss or superior that was hard to please, and if so, whether that made him feel as though the work he did was never good enough. Jack answered yes.

I then asked Jack if he always attracted relationships with women who were hard to please, who made him feel as though he was never good enough and maybe even cheated on him. Once again, Jack acknowledged this was true.

I then told Jack that I bet he also grew up with a very judgemental or criticizing parent who was hard to please and that nothing for them was ever good enough, or that he was bullied in primary school or during his teenage years.

Jack, slightly stunned, confirmed that what I had just implied about having a judgemental parent who was nearly impossible to please was spot on.

How did I know so much about Jack through the awareness of one bad shoulder and chronic neck pain? Because I know that physical reality circumstances never lie.

WHAT YOU HAVE GOING ON IS ALWAYS AN INDICATION OF YOUR VIBRATION

Back when I worked in tech, I was trained as a software architect and developer to troubleshoot problems — specifically, to identify bugs in the system which often related to patterns. Over time, I've come to identify the patterns of physical reality circumstances that relate to specific frequencies, such as the frequency of not being good enough Jack had present in his vibration.

Although reading someone's vibration in this way isn't always black and white, it's typically rooted in the same few circumstances often stemming from childhood. When someone has chronic neck and shoulder issues, for example, that's typically from emotions of stress and pressure, feeling not good enough, along with possible perfectionism tendencies. This is often a biproduct of having been raised in an environment where you were highly judged and criticized by an influential figure, having been abused, or possibly having been bullied. Although this isn't always the exact cause, it seems to be the case a majority of the time.

Being stuck sucks.

I remember over a decade ago, when, just like Jack, I felt stuck. That trapped feeling where you just can't figure out where to go or what to do next? I see it all the time, chatting with men and women during seminars or online group calls. Feeling stuck in their career, having health problems or being in bad relationship circumstances for years, if not decades, feeling totally hopeless. I'm sure one way or another, you can relate.

However, understand this.

We are never truly stuck – we simply continue to create more of the same circumstance, by emitting more of the same vibrational frequency.

Remember, you can't listen to a different station without first changing the channel you're on.

You didn't come here to just get where you are and stay there. We are ever-expanding beings that came here for the joy of growth, expansion and the discovery of new things and new experiences.

Everyone understands the law of gravity and its consistency. What you toss up, has to come back down, there are no exceptions. Law of Attraction operates with this same consistency – what vibration you put out, physical reality sends back. That's why it's called a law.

If your goal is to make alignment easy and to become a vibrational match to those things and experiences you want, you need to work on shifting out of the vibrations that are creating the resistance, holding you back from what you truly want. The ones that are always playing in the background holding you back, getting in your way, preventing your cork from naturally floating to the surface.

You've already learned about emotions, how they guide to underlying, non-serving perspectives, and how to reframe them. You can't shift out of those non-serving perspectives if you don't know they are present. So the first step is awareness. It's learning to identify what vibrations you've been practicing -- the negative, inner background noise you've stopped noticing, like the emotion of not good enough in Jack's story.

There are two specific indicators always telling you what's in your vibration, and they are never wrong.

1. The way that you feel.

2. The things going on in your physical reality.

WELCOME TO YOUR GUIDANCE SYSTEM

In our chapters about alignment, we dissected emotions. You learned about the perspectives behind them and the layered nature of these perspectives that can hold unwanted negative emotional baggage in place. The same emotional baggage that defined the frequency you emit from your attraction point.

We aren't quite done with emotions yet.

Once or twice a year Anik and I make the eight-hour trip down to Boston to attend Abraham-Hicks seminars with friends. One thing that blows my mind (other than how much fun we always have at the events, and the amazing hotseat conversations) is the crazy and confusing highways of downtown Boston. With more on- and off-ramps and forks than should ever exist in such a small stretch of highway, taking the right exit at the right time feels like blindly throwing a dart at a bullseye.

Luckily, in this modern-day and age, most vehicles and phones are equipped with a trusty GPS to guide us, letting us know exactly where to turn and when. Without it, I believe I'd still be stuck looping through the network of roads unable to find my way out.

Now, what if I told you that every single human has a built-in guidance system, an indicator telling you EXACTLY where and when you need to turn to make sure that you're on course to getting where you want to go? As a matter of fact, it's even easier to use than a GPS, because it's already pre-programmed with two ultimate destinations:

Alignment and being a vibrational match to what you want.

If GPS stands for Global Positioning System, we can call this guidance system our *Vibrational Positioning System* (VPS). Your VPS' goal is to help you position your thoughts and focus to those that match alignment, as well as the vibrational frequency of the things you want.

Want to give it a try to make sure you've got yours turned on?

First, I want you to think of your biggest accomplishment. Something you've done that makes you proud. Think about this accomplishment for a good five or six seconds, and while you do, notice how it makes you feel.

Next, I want you to think of the opposite. Just for a few seconds (really for the shortest amount of time possible - we don't want to activate that frequency too long) think of something that you may wish had never happened and notice how it makes you feel.

For the first scenario, did you feel positive, uplifting emotions? For the second scenario, did you feel more negative and unpleasant emotions? Congratulations, you've just used your VPS. Your VPS has been present as long as you've been experiencing emotions, but until this point you've just never been aware that it is in fact a guidance system. How does it work?

> **Any time you feel negative emotions, your VPS is telling you you're tuning into a non-serving perspective that is pulling you out of alignment and preventing you from being a vibrational match to what you want. Any time you feel positive emotions, your VPS is telling you you're tuning into a perspective that is congruent to alignment and a vibrational match to the desires you want.**

When you experience negative emotions, this is an indication that you're turning right when your VPS is telling you to go left. When you're experiencing positive emotions, this is your VPS signaling that you're on course for where you want to go.

Emotions – the way you feel – is the first indicator of your vibration as indicated by your VPS. The second indicator is the circumstances that present themselves to you in your physical reality.

Why?

You cannot experience that to which you are not a vibrational match to.

On the flip side, anything you are experiencing must mean you are a vibrational match to that experience, both wanted and unwanted. There is no exception to this rule, as we know that the Law of Attraction is indeed a law, like gravity.

How do we use this fact to our advantage? By using one simple question.

How does that situation or circumstance make me feel?

One of the very first exercises I do with new clients is a process to audit what's going on in their attraction point. We look at various circumstances, past and present, and look for a pattern of emotional circumstance, similar to what I did with Jack. With nearly ninety percent of men and women, a pattern of one to three emotions seems to continually emerge over the course of their life. These emotions are typically rooted in childhood or traumas and are what I call dominant negative emotions. These are the sources of resistance that, when shifted, create the most significant positive outer reality shifts both in terms of achieving alignment as well as manifestation.

The process looks something like this:

Q1: How do your financial circumstances make you feel?

A: I can't make more money show up – I feel stuck and not good enough.

Q2: What is the biggest challenge with work, and how does it make you feel?

A: I can't please my boss – he's never satisfied, and it makes me feel not good enough.

Q3: What is the biggest struggle in your relationship, and how does it make you feel?

A: I can never please them – I feel like I'm not good enough.

Q4: What was the biggest struggle in your past significant relationships, and how did it make you feel?

A: Nobody is ever there for me – it makes me feel abandoned and not good enough.

Q5: Do you butt heads with a family member? How do they make you feel?

A: They are never satisfied with how much I give or do for them – I feel powerless and not good enough.

In the above example, the person suffers from a dominant negative emotion of not good enough.

We also cross-reference the dominant emotion with physical symptoms such as neck and shoulder (not good enough), lower back (stuck/powerless), IBS (anticipation fear, walking on eggshells) because physical conditions are also manifestations with emotional root causes.

> **Each circumstance, physical condition or emotion that emerges is a bread crumb down the path to understanding what is in someone's vibration that could be standing in their way.**

If for each of these questions, you keep coming back with the same answer(s) (stuck, not good enough, anger/frustration and unworthy being some of the most common) then congratulations, you've likely identified a Dominant Negative Emotion. Working through this specific emotion through the underlying perspectives will create a significant positive shift in the way you feel and in your life.

Included in the appendix you'll find a walk-through for this process under Key Probing and Attraction Point Audit Statements.

CHAPTER KEY CONCEPT SUMMARY

- Physical reality never lies. What you have going on in your life is always an indication of what you have going on in your vibration.

- You are never stuck; you simply continue to repeat the same pattern of circumstance by continually emitting the same vibrational frequency.

- You cannot experience that with which you are not a vibrational match.

- You can't consciously shift out of a vibration if you don't know you are practicing it. The first step is identifying what you have going on in your attraction point.

- Two indicators will help you uncover what vibrations are present in your attraction point – what is going on in your physical reality, and how you feel.

- Look at patterns of circumstances and the emotions they bring up to identify what dominant negative emotions you may be carrying. Shifting out of these negative emotions will create the most significantly positive outer reality shift.

- Like a GPS, you have an internal guidance system called a Vibrational Positioning System (VPS) to guide you into alignment and toward being a vibrational match to your desires.

- Your VPS guides you to knowing what perspectives you are choosing, using emotions as an indicator. Positive emotions indicate you are on course, while negative emotions are an indicator you are off course.

7

OVERCOMING THE CURRENT REALITY LOOP

My intent for this book is to give you everything you need to reach a new level of co-creational ability so you become a master at the art of Power Manifesting. In the previous chapter, we covered vibration in great detail. In this chapter, we're going to dive even deeper so you can better understand what most people are doing wrong in the context of vibration so you can get it right.

Meet Janelle.

One of my San Francisco based clients, Janelle worked for a small-to-medium-sized tech start-up company. When Janelle first reached out to work with me, the primary focus was on love and relationships. But, being a VP of a fast-growing company, issues around work became a reoccurring theme, centering around a problematic HR manager.

First, he tried to withhold a bonus she was entitled to. Second, he was causing issues around a compensation plan she was promised when she was first hired. Third, he was trying to rally her team of employees against her while she was away on business trips in New York.

Janelle's immediate reaction to each of these circumstances? Like most people, it was to put up a fight. To call the CEO, arrange meetings with other VPs, write a report, seek justification, most of which she had tried over a number of months, but she kept hitting brick wall after brick wall.

Janelle had been pushing against these issues and the HR manager for months, yet no progress was ever being made.

In one of our sessions, I convinced Janelle to take a vibrational approach to these problems. We looked at what was in her vibration, we did some perspective reframing and clearing work, and I instructed her to let it all go and stop pushing against the problem. To not do anything to resolve the problem, but simply stay off the topic and work on embodying where she wanted to be if everything were to work out for her.

Over the coming weeks, like magic, things started to shift.

She was finally awarded her bonus (completely out of the blue).

Talks were re-initiated around the compensation plan.

And, the problematic HR manager who was the figurative thorn in her side, who was bad-mouthing her and getting in the way of the things she believed she rightfully deserved? Other employees also came forward with issues, and he resigned his position and moved on to work for a different company.

What was the clincher that allowed this new unfolding to take place? Part of it was her being in alignment. Part of it was clearing the resistance in her vibration around struggle and unworthiness. But, the bigger part, was her making her way out of the energy and vibration of the problem, which freed up the energy, allowing these shifts to take place.

Up until this point, the dominant focus on the topic of alignment and vibration has centered around emotions and their underlying perspectives. But this isn't the only thing that impacts what's in your attraction point and manifestation. The other major factor you need to take into consideration is where you put your focus.

YOU GET WHAT YOU FOCUS ON WHETHER YOU WANT IT OR NOT

Have you ever tried manifesting a specific type of car? Maybe a nice Mercedes or a Range Rover? Have you ever noticed that when you begin to put your focus on that specific vehicle, you begin to see it everywhere you go?

A few years ago, I was doing one of my favorite summer activities, lying in the sun while enjoying the cool ocean breeze. On this July afternoon I was on a lounger on my patio, listening to the waves gently beating on the shoreline, with a journal on my lap, plugging away at a common exercise I assign to many of my clients.

That day I had chosen to practice the vibration of abundance (the opposite vibration of lack). In my journal, I was writing something that looked like this.

I am abundant. Abundance. That feeling of abundance. I am abundant. I am abundant. I am abundant. Abundance. The abundance of oxygen for me to breath. The abundance of sunshine on my skin. The abundance of sand on the beach. Abundance. Abundance. Abundance. Abundance. I am abundant.

With each word, just as I instruct my clients, I made sure I experienced that feeling of abundance radiating from my chest, my solar plexus, expanding outwards from my whole body. I was tuning my receiver to that vibrational frequency.

After about seven to ten minutes of practicing this exercise, Anik came outside, asking me if I was interested in going for a walk up and down the beach, something we do often in the summertime, almost daily, weather permitting. I put my journal down and decided to join her.

Ours is the last beachfront home on a small stretch of beach; at the other end is a small wharf, mainly used for pleasure boats and lobster fishing boats. At a nice relaxed pace, it typically takes about fifteen minutes to walk from one end of the beach to the other. On the typical up and down, we'll often find a few pieces of sea glass, no more than four or five, maybe six or seven on a good day.

Today was different.

After doing our usual up and down the beach, as I walked back up the steps towards the patio, both Anik and I each literally had both hands overflowing with sea glass, it felt like ten times more than we've ever found at once. Although this was a surprise, it was also unexpected, until I realized I had set my intent and put my focus, right up until our walk on the beach, on fine-tuning my vibration and tapping into the frequency of abundance.

I like telling the beach glass story because it shows that vibration applies to more than just stuff – it also applied to states such as ease, abundance, freedom, clarity and satisfaction. These are all vibrational frequencies that you can practice and tune into.

Janelle's story and my beach glass experience are examples of how the focus you put out will begin to shift your reality and attract something you may be giving your attention to. It can be a car, more abundance or really any thing or aspect in your physical reality. This understanding can actively be used for your benefit, by consciously giving focus to the things you want. But, if you're like most people, the art of where you put your focus is working against you.

Here's where things get complicated. Any time you notice the presence of a desire, you're practicing the vibrational frequency of that desire being present in your physical reality. This is a step in the right direction.

Any time you notice the lack of presence of a desire, its absence, you're activating the vibrational frequency of that desire's being absent from your physical reality. This is a step in the wrong direction.

Let's suppose the unfolding of the manifestation of your desire was represented by a ten-meter-long stick where the leftmost side represented absence, while the rightmost side represents manifestation. You begin in the middle of the stick, at the halfway point, and your goal is to reach the right end of the stick, at which point manifestation will occur.

Every time you have a thought about the desire that feels good and brings excitement, and focus in such a way where you embody the presence of the desire, or embody what the solution would feel like, you take a step towards the right side of the stick, towards manifestation.

Every time you notice the absence of the desire, and focus on the problem or focus on the desire in such a way that triggers negative emotion, you're taking a step towards the left side of the stick, away from manifestation.

REALITY GOES WHERE YOUR ATTENTION FLOWS

This may sound like Law of Attraction 101, but this is a major stumbling block for most people, and here's why.

Human beings are problem addicts. You could have ten different things going amazingly well in your life with one thing going wrong. If you're like most people, you put most of your time, energy, and focus trying to solve that one thing going wrong. You give most of your attention to it. We want things to be perfect and if anything falls outside that norm, we believe we need to do something to fix it.

How does this impact our point of focus and what sits in our attraction point? We add momentum to unwanted circumstances because we continually focus on them. This is what I call the *current reality loop*.

Have you ever noticed that when riding a bike if you turn and look towards the left, you'll automatically steer and head into that direction? Or, if you are looking right, the bike will go right? When you continually give focus in one direction, you will move towards it. If you got on a bike in a large area, kept at the same speed looking in the same direction, to the left, you would continue to turn in a circle. You would continue to spin around and end up where you started.

> **By constantly observing the same thing in your physical reality, usually by staying focused on the problem, you're propagating that cycle, creating more of the same reality.**

The more you put focus on what you have going on, the more momentum you give to drawing in more of that circumstance. You spin in a circle and keep ending up back in the problem. Sometimes, if you're pushing harder and harder against it, it's like you pedal the bike harder and harder, and you keep coming back to the starting point faster. You feel more stuck, and the problem gets worse.

How do we escape? You need to interrupt the pattern by shifting away from the problem long enough, putting your focus dominantly on something you prefer – a new direction – to exit this current reality loop and head in a new direction.

How do we do this? Get out ahead of the problem by putting more focus on where you want to be rather than where you currently are. If your bike is continually spinning in a circle because you face left, you need to face towards the right. You can do this by committing to spend time every day daydreaming about the outcome you prefer. Or, even better, practice embodiment.

If daydreaming were represented by a ten-mile jog, embodiment would be the equivalent to a ten-mile sprint. Like daydreaming, in an embodiment process, we put focus on our desire from a present-tense state as if we already have it. What would it feel like if you had that desire, right here, right now? How would your desire taste or smell? What would it feel like if you touched it? What colors do you see when you look at it? How do you feel, now that you have it?

There are multiple ways you can practice the act of embodiment. Here are a few exercises from a process called The Into Existence Process which I've given to members of The Power Manifesting Collective – my group membership program. I've shared the entire process with you in the appendix of this book.

Write it into existence – Write about the desire, pen or pencil on paper, in the present tense, as if you already have it.

Speak it into existence – Speak about the desire, out loud, in the present tense, as if you already have it.

Dream it into existence – Visualize and tune into the desire with all five senses in the present tense, as if you already have it. I have recorded a guided meditation audio available for this process in the bonus companion content at http:// nickbreau.com/bonus.

Live it into existence – This is a process where you spend segments of your day acting out of the energy of already having that desire. Want to manifest forty million dollars? When you make coffee, practice what it would feel like to make coffee as a forty millionaire. Gassing up your car? What does it feel like to gas up being a forty millionaire? Heading to the washroom so you can empty your bladder? You get the point.

When it comes to desire embodiment, the only rule is, the more detailed you get and the stronger the positive emotion you're able to generate, the greater the impact this process will have.

In Janelle's case, the shift was quick and obvious once she took the right action – action from a vibrational standpoint. If you were to ask her what the biggest challenge was, she likely would have told you that taking time to do embodiment each day was the easy part. The harder part was letting go.

Over the next few chapters, we'll be exploring these topics, letting go (allowing) and action taking, in greater detail to help you make similar shifts in letting in the things you want, as demonstrated by Janelle.

CHAPTER KEY CONCEPT SUMMARY

- Vibrational frequency applies to more than just things – it applies to experiences such as ease, effortlessness and abundance.

- Where you put your focus matters. Reality flows where your attention goes.

- I AM are the two most powerful words in the English language, because of the vibrational frequency that matches what follows these words.

- Most people are manifesting by default, experiencing more of the same because they continually observe what is – and so, create more of what is. This is called the current reality loop.

- Use daydreaming as a tool to interrupt the loop (a pattern interrupt), to get out ahead of what is and create more of what you really want.

- Use the embodiment processes to help become a vibrational match to your desires. Do this by speaking, writing, acting out as if (living), and dreaming about those desires.

ALLOWING

8

HOW TO SURRENDER AND THE ART OF LETTING GO

In the context of the Law of Attraction and manifestation, I believed for a long time that the subject of allowing was around allowing your desires to come to you and staying out of the energy of effort. Over time, I realized that allowing applies to much more than that. In fact, I've broken the subject down into three distinct topics.

1. Allowing desires to come to you – in other words, not chasing after them.

2. Allowing contrast – not pushing against the unwanted circumstances in your life.

3. Allowing absence – not pushing against the fact that something you really want has not yet shown up.

EVERYTHING I WANT IS CHASING ME

In the fall of 2018, I spent a week on the beautiful and magical Spanish island of Mallorca, located in the middle of the Mediterranean near Ibiza. This was my second trip to this island and I had rented an Airbnb in which I assembled a handful of friends and team members.

When it comes to travel destinations, good food, sun, and beaches are at the top of my priority list. When I first visited Mallorca with Anik a few years prior, we found some amazing beaches as well as some great food, including my favorite dessert, tiramisu. On this trip, I had my sights on more of the same.

On the second day with my team members, I made one of the most important decisions of the entire trip. I decided that this week, while in Mallorca, I would have the best tiramisu of my entire life. Not only, that, but I also decided that it was going to find me.

Over the course of the trip, here and there, I would repeat that statement, that my piece of tiramisu already existed, and it was chasing me.

One day walking around town we walked by a fancy ice cream shop, one of the women exclaimed, "Look, Nick, the first one on the menu is tiramisu ice cream!" Nope, I wanted tiramisu, not ice cream, so that wasn't it.

The next day we walked by a popular Italian restaurant and the group suggested I go in and see if they had tiramisu on the menu. Once again, I implied that I wasn't chasing after it – that it was going to find me.

Another day we spent the afternoon at a beach club that also had tiramisu, this time strawberry tiramisu, but this wasn't it either. I stayed patient and firmly stood my energetic ground that I was going to have the best tiramisu, and it would find me.

Then, the second to last night, it finally happened. Anik and I decided to have an evening out alone, and we followed our inspiration to an amazing restaurant called Quina Creu. After our appetizers, the main course and some wine, we were absolutely stuffed. I felt like I couldn't take another bite. The waiter came around asking about dessert, and just as I was about to say no, thank you, a part of me hesitated in my response. I held back. I felt a split-second intuitive nudge about seeing the dessert menu, so I said sure, why not (by this point in the trip I had actually forgotten about the tiramisu request I had set out at the beginning of the week).

The waiter shortly disappeared around the corner and as he returned from about fifteen feet away, I could see, in the top right corner of the tray amongst seven or eight other things, the biggest, most delicious-looking piece of tiramisu I have ever laid my eyes upon (you can actually find a picture of it on my Facebook page).

As he approached the table he said, "And the very first thing I have here, is tiramisu, and next, we have …" and I immediately cut him off. "That's it." I said it without even giving him a chance to show us what else was on the tray. "That's my piece of tiramisu, I'll have that please."

That piece of tiramisu was without a doubt the best piece I have, to this day, ever had. It was so good in fact that we went back a second night with our friends for a second helping. The best part? Just as I had originally set my intent, there was no seeking out the tiramisu. It came to me.

This experience led to my favorite new affirmation "Everything I want is chasing me," which has also inspired an audio mashup available on my YouTube channel (http://youtube.com/nickbreau)

The art of allowing doesn't only apply to what we perceive as little things such as tiramisu. Allowing applies to all desires, big and small. Learning to become a master allower is one of the steps that leads to power manifesting.

What is the greatest dis-allower of allowing? Effort. Trying to force the process by taking too much action in order to make things show up.

We'll explore this in detail as we visit the next section – Action. For now, understand that all desire can potentially arrive with the same ease as the tiramisu has for me, from that pure place of allowing, non-resistance and non-effort. It's not your job to take care of how things are going to show up – that's not up to you. Your job is to line up vibrationally with what you want and allow that desire to come to you.

ALLOWING THE UNWANTED

The second of our three elements of allowing is learning to allow the contrast we've attracted in our life. As explained in the previous chapter, when we manifest unwanted circumstances our natural tendency is to push against them, resulting in a current reality loop and giving more momentum to the unwanted.

What steps can we take to be more allowing of the unwanted? First, acknowledge that you created it and you didn't screw up.

> **Own it. By owning it you take responsibility for it, and since you created it, you are empowered to uncreate it.**

You can't change what you don't own. You cannot experience what is not a match to your vibration. If it's in your physical reality, it has to be a match to your vibration. If you don't feel like you own it, you're placing yourself in a vibrationally powerless place, believing that something outside of you is in control and over which you may not have power, which is a false and limiting perception.

On that same topic, you aren't being punished and you didn't screw up. Humans have a tendency to want to label things as good or bad, obviously good being wanted, bad being unwanted. But the reality is that there is no good or bad, just preference. Seeing a circumstance as non-preferential, rather than bad, will take some of its power away.

Which of these two states feels lighter to you?

"Oh no, I don't want this, this is bad, quick, I need to fix this" vs, "Oh, look at that, I created something I do not prefer, I guess I'll create something different."

By shifting your perspective in this way, you stop seeing the negative as negative. The end result is less pushing against and a greater state of letting go.

Second, understand that you are being presented with an opportunity.

Physical reality and the source energy behind it is infinitely intelligent. Everything that ever has or ever will exist, has purpose. Even if you don't yet see the purpose of the contrast you may be experiencing, it doesn't mean it's not an opportunity for growth and expansion.

> **Contrast is always an opportunity for growth and expansion with the potential to lead you to more of what you want.**

Again, which of these two states feels lighter to you?

"Oh no, another hole I need to dig myself out of" vs. "How exciting, a new breadcrumb along the trail of learning to become a better focuser and better creator, leading me to more of what I want."

Third, take action – the right action.

The old paradigm response to contrast is to jump into effort and action. What's the solution to this problem? How do I solve it? Who do I call or what actions do I take to fix this? The new paradigm response? More contrast, how exciting! Another breadcrumb, a hint to help me learn more about what I have going on in my vibration so I can shift in ways that bring me closer to what I really want.

When in the face of contrast, from the new paradigm vantage point, the proper action isn't physical reality-based action, but internal action. It's about shifting the way you think and feel so that it's no longer a match to this physical reality circumstance you do not prefer. We'll discuss the topic of action-taking from a vibrational vantage point in the next chapter.

So how should you respond to the contrast?

Observe it. Allow it. Acknowledge the discomfort as the guidance that it is. You can also use the following question to dig into what perspectives you may have going on that could be causing this.

> *What must I believe to be true, in order for this circumstance to manifest into my reality?*

Was it fear? Was it an emotion with an underlying perspective? Was it too much focus on a problem?

CONTRAST - BY YOU FOR YOU

Have you ever reflected on how an unconditionally loving parent would treat their child in the face of contrast? When my son was learning to tie his shoes and in a rush to get outside and play with his friends or catch up with his sister, he'd get impatient, angry, and upset.

I can understand his anger and frustration towards me and his little piece of contrast, rushing and struggling to get his shoes tied. Wishing he could just snap his fingers and be done with it. I could understand his anger towards me, as he knows that I could just bend over and do it for him. At the young age of four or five, he doesn't understand the purpose of me not interfering and doing it for him.

As a parent, I can do two things.

One, I could just do it for him, over and over again. But, would he ever learn? How would he feel as a teenager still unable to tie his shoes since his dad followed him around and did it for him his whole life?

Or two, I could step back, allow the contrast of the circumstance to unfold so that it plays out in a way that teaches him how to learn, grow, and expand, and become competent in shoe-tying.

In his four- or five-year-old mind, he doesn't see how the contrast is serving him, even though I do. As the unconditionally loving father, as hard as it is to watch my son struggle and not want him to struggle, I know this contrast is in his best interest.

Shoe-tying may be a simple form of contrast (and as an adult, not a very painful one), but the same analogy applies to adult circumstances and adult contrast.

The perspective I like to choose, in the face of contrast, which helps me let go, is that I'm an extension of source energy. An extension of infinite intelligence. My belief is that infinite intelligence can create anything, it can put me in any circumstance possible. Infinite intelligence, like a caring parent, is also unconditionally loving. If it can create anything and has my best interests in mind, then who am I to doubt the experiences it has allowed me to co-create with it? Who am I to doubt or push against an experience that is being created for me by infinite intelligence? Of all the things it can create, if I find myself here, this must be the absolute best circumstance for me and my evolution.

> **In the same way I allow my son to experience contrast for his own growth, my inner being, and source energy, allow me to experience contrast for my own growth.**

The more you become okay with this contrast, the less you push against it and activate the vibration of it. The less you activate its vibration, the faster you'll move through the unwanted toward where you really want to be.

The third and final puzzle piece in the context of allowing is learning to allow when something you strongly desire has not yet arrived.

THE ART OF DETACHMENT AND LETTING GO

Learning how to let go is one of the most-discussed topics, and sometimes one of the most challenging things to do, when it comes to manifestation. Why is it that for some desires, letting go is so hard, and how does it get in the way of allowing the things you want to show up in your reality?

What is the opposite of the state of having let go? Desperation. The more you feel a need for something, the more desperate you are to have this thing you really want, and the harder it is for you to let it go. Those who struggle with impatience should listen up as well, as impatience is very similar to the energy of desperation or need.

You are noticing the absence of the thing you desire. That yucky feeling of desperation, and absence of the desired, is an indicator that you are focused in opposition to what you want, and every single time you focus on the absence of it, what are you doing? You're pushing it away by practicing the vibration of lack. That's why desperation feels so bad, and that's why it gets in the way of manifestation.

> **Every time you practice the vibration of desperation or impatience, you practice the vibration of "I don't have that thing I want."**

What causes desperation?

Discomfort due to the absence of the thing you desire. But, why the desperation around that specific desire? Because you have an emotional wound or feeling you are looking to soothe through this desire.

Take Gina for example. I've frequently worked with men and women who seek my help in overcoming a past breakup or want to re-attract an ex-partner. They are obsessed with being in a relationship with one single person and they have a false perception that nobody else could ever compare to that one person they are after. Without them, they feel miserable and would do almost anything to have them back.

When Gina came to me, she had felt miserable since no longer being in a relationship with Johnathan, who had broken up with her over a year ago. Without him in her life, she said, life felt as though it had very little meaning.

What Gina and most people fail to realize, is that it isn't Johnathan she's after. It's the underlying feelings of connection, being desired, and worth she felt while in the relationship. Because she had never received these states from anyone Gina's brain associated those emotional states with Johnathan. Since Gina only knew those emotions through that one person, her subconscious mind made the mistake of believing he was the only one who could ever soothe her emotions of feeling unworthy and undesired. Hence, the root cause of her desperation.

> **What most people fail to see is that it isn't the desire we're chasing – we're chasing how we believe we will feel once we have that desire. We're looking to soothe a negative emotional state. The more intensely we feel that negative emotion, the greater the need, impatience or desperation we have toward wanting that desire to show up.**

We want money for relief, ease, and freedom. Relationships, to feel loved, connected, worthy and good enough. That promotion, to feel validated and successful.

In order to effectively deal with desperation and impatience, you need to soothe the underlying emotional reason you're chasing after that thing you want. You need to deal with the underlying negative emotions.

Is there a specific desire you've been chasing for a very long time, where you're experiencing a strong feeling of need, desperation or impatience? Ask yourself, how would I feel if I had that which I desire? What core positive emotions would it bring? These are the feelings you need to reach for and make your dominant state. The negative counterparts of these emotions are also likely the dominant negative emotions creating the resistance preventing you from being a vibrational match. Dealing with these will not only help the impatience and desperation, but they'll also help with your vibration.

How do you know if you've achieved this?

You feel so good, you're so happy, that you don't care that the sense of desire is absent anymore. When you achieve this state, like clockwork, that's almost always when the thing you desire shows up.

A quick tip to ensure you're in the right energy on the topic of desperation is checking in with yourself to see if you're in a state of want and need, or in a state of desiring. Take a moment to tune into those words. Which feels lighter to you? Which feels heavier and more constrictive? The state of desiring should feel lighter and more relaxed than want or need. If you find yourself dominantly in want or need, you may want to do a bit of work to ease your way into the state of desire.

Another exercise you can put into practice that can assist you in letting go is using an avatar.

A few months ago Anik was visiting her mom when her aunt dropped by to say hello. Anik was aware that her aunt was planning to sell her house to move into a maintenance-free condominium. Anik asked if she had any potential buyers yet. Sounding discouraged, her aunt shared that over the last four months she had less than a handful of visits and zero serious interest.

That's when Anik suggested that she do what she had done years ago to sell her house – bury a statue of Saint Joseph upside down in a flowerbed in the front yard. This is common long-time superstition in our area that I had heard once before, which suggests that by burying the statue in this way, your house will sell quickly and with ease.

With nothing to lose, her aunt proceeded as Anik told her, and no more than seven days later, after over three months with no momentum, the house sold.

Why does this superstition work for so many people? Is Saint Joseph sitting behind the scenes in the nonphysical waiting to jump into action and sell homes? Not really. What's happening at an energetic level is you are handing off the process and responsibility to someone (or something) else. You're energetically letting go and releasing the responsibility of being the one that needs to make things happen. You're shifting yourself to a vibration of relief.

A task I gave to the students in one of my group money-coaching programs was to choose for themselves an avatar representing their inner being or nonphysical energy, that could take over and manage any task for them. I told them they could choose a Saint (similar to Saint Joseph), a god or goddess, anything really that they felt would accurately represent the infinitely powerful nonphysical energy guiding and supporting them. I chose a Yoda bobblehead.

What you decide to choose doesn't matter. What does matter is what it represents for you, and that you feel comfortable handing over to it the responsibility of making things happen. Any desire that comes to mind – whether it be to sell a house, to manifest a relationship, to deliver a job or money – write it down on a small piece of paper or sticky note, then hand it over to your avatar by placing that paper in front or under it, like placing an order into the universe.

One final point around the topic of allowing and letting go is to not forget about the old and new paradigms. If you're chasing a desire, you may be stuck in the old paradigm of needing to achieve and make something happen. When you fully embrace the new paradigm of being and allowing, where alignment and feeling good is the focus, the state of allowing becomes more inherent because you simply feel good.

CHAPTER KEY CONCEPT SUMMARY

- Effort is the greatest dis-allower of allowing – the energy of effort is one of the dominant energies that prevents manifestation.

- When unwanted circumstances present themselves in our lives, we have a tendency to want to jump into effort and action to counter them. Instead, allow the circumstances to play out while investigating and taking action from an internal vibrational standpoint.

- We can't change what we don't own. Own your reality and acknowledge that you're just as responsible for the unwanted, as you are the wanted. By owning your contrast, you are stepping to an empowered place where you can change your unwanted circumstances.

- The more you are okay and not pushing against the contrast that presents itself, the faster you will move through it.

- The struggle in allowing comes from the dependence on specific desires to achieve emotional states. Allowing becomes easy when we realize these emotional states are achievable without the desire. Once we break free from this dependence, the things we desire tend to show up.

- Being dependent on desires and practicing need puts us in the vibration of lack, therefore creating momentum in the wrong direction.

- Want and need are resistant states congruent to desperation; the ideal state to be in is desire, rather than want or need.

- In order to practice letting go and stepping out of effort, choose an avatar that represents your inner being or the nonphysical to which you can give over responsibility. This will assist you in the letting go process.

- From a place of pure allowingness and non-resistance, recognize that everything you want is chasing you.

ACTION

9

HOW TO KICK THE HABIT OF EFFORT AND STRUGGLE

I love synchronicities. The big, the small. It's part of what truly exemplifies the magic of our life experience when we really step into the power of co-creation and alignment.

One of my favorite stories of synchronicity, one that I tell often, is that of my current relationship with Anik.

A number of months after I had separated from my marriage, I found myself at a weekend workshop studying meditation and sacred geometry with a few friends. That Saturday night, after a day of meditation and other exercises, I was hanging out with my friend, Sophie. Shortly after I had arrived at her place, I got a text from a good friend, Dan. He asked if I wanted to join him and his friend and share some of the insights from our workshop that day. I was a bit saturated of spiritual talk, and part of me felt like I needed a break, but an inner nudge was giving me the impulse to go. Dan gave me his friend's address where we could find them, and then Sophie and I hopped into the car and headed out.

Upon arriving, Dan greeted us at the door and welcomed us in. We headed to the living room where he introduced us to his beautiful, bright-eyed and very attractive friend, Anik.

We spent most of the night talking about sacred geometry as well as the spiritual topic of Twin Flames. I was curious about Anik (and why Dan – who I had been friends with for a while – had never introduced us before). Although there was no immediate and obvious connection with Anik, we had a great night with some fantastic conversation, before heading home sometime after midnight.

After dropping off Sophie and getting home that evening, I saw that Anik had sent me a Facebook friend request. We chatted some more and decided to meet up again the following night. We continued to hang out and our connection grew. We've now been together as a couple for nearly seven years. In my forty years of existence, I've never met someone with whom I share such compatibility. Even though we are different in many ways, we've never had an argument. We're both always on the same page and share all the same interests. It is by far the easiest and most flowing and satisfying relationship I've had, or even thought possible.

Want to know what else? If you hadn't noticed, we share very similar names, Nick and Anik. We both do the same type of spiritual and personal development coaching work. When we met, we both drove the exact same make and model of vehicle. And, after a few months of dating, we realized we had both left our marriages on the exact same day, before we had ever met. Now, even though this is a great story and a beautiful tale of synchronicity, what does this have to do with action? There's literally no talk of action-taking in this story whatsoever, other than following the impulse to meet with Dan, even when my mind tried to talk me out of it.

That's the point.

Hypothetically, let's say that before Anik and I had ever met, I somehow already knew she existed. That somewhere out there, there is an ideal match for me, a twin, who shares amazing synchronicities and would be the absolute most perfect partner for me.

With over 7 billion humans inhabiting this planet, where would I even begin to try to find her? Would I start with Tinder? Would I place an ad in every newspaper on the planet? Would I start putting missing-person-type posters on telephone poles all around the world?

If you knew your ideal match was somewhere out there, what action would you take to ensure you would find that person?

The reality is that there is no action you, in your physical form, can take to ensure finding that person. In fact, if you're like most people, the action you take is efforted action that will result in vibrationally pushing that person even further away and creating momentum in the wrong direction.

The only way you can line up with this needle in a haystack is to let your inner being do the work and lead you there. It's to allow the infinite intelligence of source, who is all knowing and has a solution to every problem, to guide you to that desire from an aligned place. To allow it to lead you, using inspired action typically through the form of excitement and impulse.

If you look back on your life, how often have you noticed that when you seemingly give up on something, when you stop looking for it or trying to make it happen through effort, it shows up? That's because from an energetic standpoint, you are stepping out of effort and into allowing.

Any time you are taking effort-based action, you are cutting yourself off from alignment because you are tuning into lack, or the absence of that desire.

Think about what it's like when you forget the name of a person or a place, for example, and you are trying to recall it on the spot. You keep repeating to yourself "What is that name again? Why can't I remember it, it's on the tip of my tongue." Moments later you give up, stop thinking about it, and then later, when you're completely off the topic, the name pops into your head.

Effort is one of, if not the, dominant cause for a kink in our manifesting hose. We live in a society that glorifies effort and hard work. If you want to be somebody in life, if you want to accomplish big things, if you want to have lots of money and be successful, it all takes hard work and effort. If there was one limiting belief that we could pluck out of society like a bad weed, I would choose this one.

So why, under the context of manifestation, is effort getting in our way?

> **When we're in the energy of effort, we're putting out the vibrational frequency of "My desire is not here" – a vibration of absence of that desire.**

Action from a place of effort reinforces this vibration, which, in turn, creates a bigger gap between it and your experience of it. It pulls you away from being a vibrational match.

Over the last few years I've worked with a number of coaches in a variety of niches who struggle to attract clients. In over eighty percent of these cases, one of the following two issues was the dominant cause of their lack of client attraction.

1. The fear of putting themselves out there (we'll talk more about fears and split energy in an upcoming chapter)

2. Being stuck in the energy of effort.

One of the very first questions I ask, is how many hours a day are you putting into your business? The typical answer is eight to twelve hours. Our automatic response to a problem we want to solve is to increase our level of effort and oftentimes these coaches are on the verge of burning out.

I also ask, when you're not at work, is your mind still focused on the business and how to bring in more clients? What ads to create, what videos to shoot, what articles to publish? The answer is often yes, and, unfortunately, mental effort, even if just sitting in your living room thinking about your business, is still fueling the energy of effort and vibration of lack of clients.

The very first piece of homework I give these clients? Take a break.

I give them the permission, outside of scheduled calls with their clients, to work on their business for a maximum of two hours a day. The rest of their day is to be spent chilling out and having fun. Go to the beach. Ride your bike. Binge watch a show on Netflix. Go do something fun and exciting that feels good, and most importantly, stay off the topic of your business, because otherwise you're re-activating the vibration of lack.

Most people struggle when I tell them to take no action. To go have fun and to be lazy. Yes, your read that right. Go be lazy.

DELIBERATELY DOING NOTHING IS DOING SOMETHING

Our perception is that lazy is bad. Lazy is unproductive. The truth? Being lazy is one of the most productive things you can do. Why? Because being lazy is **VIBRATIONALLY PRODUCTIVE.**

We see effort and hard work as being productive, because we don't understand, or forget about, the law of attraction and the vibrational nature of reality.

> **True productivity comes from alignment. It comes from feeling good because from that place of feeling good, relaxation, satisfaction, happiness, fun; we stand in our power.**

Another one of my favorite terms, is **VROI - Vibrational Return on Investment.**

Spring has started to shift into summer here and the cold frosty mornings have finally given way, allowing me to get started on our vegetable garden. In anticipation of all the tomatoes, peppers, squash, cucumbers and other veggies we plant every year, we visited and picked up everything we needed at the local greenhouse last week, nearly two hundred dollars in transplants and seeds.

At first, my inner critic started to knock on my door, implying this was a lot of money to spend on a garden. But I reassured it that all the vegetables the garden would grow by fall would have a positive return on investment as we wouldn't need to spend money on expensive, organic vegetables at the grocery store. This made sense to my inner critic and it was now convinced that it was a smart purchase, so it left me alone.

A few days later, we visited another greenhouse, this time looking for a few flowers to landscape with around the yard.

As we went down each row exploring all the different types of flowers, our tray was getting more and more full. We eventually headed to the cash register with two giant trays filled with annuals. What's an "annual," you might wonder? An annual is a flower that only lasts one season. At the end of the season (which is only about four months here in Canada), the flower dies, never to be seen again. In other words, an annual is a flower that my inner critic sees as a waste of money.

Once again, my inner critic tried launching another assault. "What are you thinking? Why would you spend money on something that will simply die in a matter of months, giving you nothing in return? You are just throwing your money away."

At first, I started to worry, as I was spending close to the same amount of money on these annuals as I had spent on the vegetables. I was almost convinced by my inner critic that I was throwing money away. But then, I was given a very important insight by my inner being.

After the harsh Canadian winter, I like to spend as much time outside as possible. Living on the beach, we spend hours each day lying in the sand or on our deck overlooking the ocean as well as the flowerbeds around the yard.

What kind of an impact will a beautifully landscaped yard have on the way I feel, from a vibrational standpoint? Tall yellow and red sunflowers, giant colorful dahlias, rows of tulips all attracting beautiful butterflies and hummingbirds. Overlooking a yard filled with beauty, spending hours in appreciation for these flowers and the beauty of nature doesn't just give me something pretty to look at. It shifts me into a higher vibrational state, which allows me higher levels of alignment, and it puts me more in the receptive mode, which translates into my reality bringing me more of what I want.

> **Spending money on these flowers isn't a waste at all, as it provides an extremely high return on investment – a Vibrational Return on Investment. No investment will yield better results and a better return, than something that helps you feel good and puts you in alignment.**

If you want to become a leading edge co-creator and master the art of power manifesting, drop the idea that action, founded in effort and hard work, is what matters. Shift into the mindset that alignment and vibrational productivity are what matter most.

UNDERSTANDING THE TWO TYPES OF ACTION

On the topic of action, it all boils down to this.

There are two types of action: efforted action (matching the old paradigm of being), and inspired action (matching the new paradigm of being).

Efforted Action is the type of action that you take because you want to achieve a goal by trying to make things happen.

Inspired or Aligned Action is the type of action that comes from being in alignment, as an impulse.

How do you tell the difference?

If you're acting solely as a means to achieve a specific result, if you're acting not for the fun of the action, but for an outcome, odds are the action is out of effort. Ask yourself – if this action didn't result in the desired outcome, would I still take it? If the answer is no, then odds are you're acting out of effort.

If you're acting because that action step feels exciting, because it feels good; if it's a hell yes, I can't not take this action; if you're taking the action for the joy of the action regardless of the end result, from an aligned place – then odds are this action is inspired action.

Inspired action often shows up as sudden ideas or impulses, while efforted action is typically the result of being focused on and in the energy of the problem.

Aligned and inspired action will typically take you further along your path, closer to what you really want. Efforted action is seemingly productive from the inner critic's standpoint (who measures results and productivity through effort), but true progress is made vibrationally.

How do you make and measure vibrational progress? You make it by doing the things that feel good and are fun, and you measure it solely by how good you feel.

What does this look like in the context of the old versus the new paradigm? See below. As you read through these points, you may want to ask yourself how much you operate in the old versus the new.

Old Paradigm	New Paradigm
• Hard work creates results. • Study harder, put in more effort, put in more hours to achieve your goals and success. • Keep grinding and hustling. • I act out of effort. • I am always pushing against and in the energy of the problem.	• My productivity is measured by how good I feel. • Laziness, relaxation, satisfaction and feeling good are true means of productivity. • The more I am aligned and the more I relax, the more I am in the receptive mode and the more my desires come to me. • I act out of inspired impulses that feel good. • I stay in the energy of the solution.

Living in a society that dominantly glorifies hard work and effort, shifting into the new paradigm of action taking is one of the most challenging aspects of mastering the art of Power Manifesting. How *dare* you embrace adding laziness, fun and play, and even afternoon naps, into your schedule when you have a lawn to mow or a report to finish?

We're so ingrained in the habit of needing to work hard and accomplish things, that our rational mind may even have a tough time prioritizing the activities that feel good, as it can't directly correlate how lying on the beach is more productive than creating ads, blogposts and videos. I still find myself on many occasions falling back in the pattern of effort when in fact I shouldn't be.

You won't become a master at embracing the new paradigm action-taking overnight. It will take time not only to develop a new habit, but to convince your mind that vibrational earning is in fact, the most productive earning type of all. How do you help convince the mind? The only real means is life experience. I can tell you hundreds of stories of incredible synchronicities and yet, until you truly begin to experience and see the benefits for yourself, your mind will continue to push against it with disbelief.

My advice is this.

Give it one month. One month of living life in alignment, reminding yourself every morning, to make vibrational earning a priority over effort and hard work, and see what happens. The more you begin to experience the benefits, the more your mind will ease into this new understanding. The more you ease into this understanding, the deeper the transition you'll make into the new paradigm of existence and the greater the step you'll take towards Power Manifesting.

CHAPTER KEY CONCEPT SUMMARY

- Inaction is the greatest form of action. The greatest way to manifest desires is from a place of alignment inspired action provided by your inner being.

- Inspired action from a place of alignment is the empowered action-taking you want, rather than efforted action which is disconnected from inner being guidance.

- Efforted action activates the vibration of lack, once again creating momentum towards absence rather than manifestation.

- Effort isn't only about physical action; it's also mental energetic action.

- Lazy is perceived as bad in society, yet it is extremely vibrationally productive and leads to inspired action. The most powerful and productive action you can take is action that boosts the way you feel. Think in terms of Vibrational Productivity and Vibrational Return on Investment.

- Recognize efforted action as action you're taking to accomplish a goal or a result. Inspired action is action you take simply because that action feels good, regardless of outcome.

- Measure your vibrational productivity based on how good you feel.

10

A PRACTICAL GUIDE TO ALIGNED ACTION TAKING

So far in the context of action-taking, we've talked about what truly results in productivity. How action fueled by effort holds you back, and how action should be taken instead out of inspiration and alignment – that the best guidance comes when we feel good.

So how do we put it all together in a practical way to make sure you're maximizing your time and achieving your full potential as an aligned action taker? I'm going to tell you exactly how to do that.

The first step – which should be obvious by now – is getting into alignment. If you're not in alignment it's going to be difficult to receive those impulses and inner guidance from your inner being. Action out of inspiration is much more difficult from that disconnected place. In the state of alignment your intuition, and those inspired impulses, come through loud and clear.

Have you ever given much thought to where intuition or these impulses come from?

I never really questioned it most of my life, ruling it out as coincidence or lucky guesses until one day about fifteen years ago. Sometime just after 8 A.M., in the middle of the week, I was on my way to work, just a typical weekday morning. After crossing the bridge that separates the north and south sides of town, I started heading down the left lane of a two-lane one-way street, in a semi-residential area.

All of a sudden, without any rhyme or reason, I had an unshakeable, unignorable urge to swerve immediately into the other lane, which I did without hesitation before my mind even had a chance to kick in and comprehend the impulse. As I made a hard cut to swing into the other lane, a vehicle pulled out from behind a hedge, without looking for any oncoming traffic at all.

If I hadn't had the impulse to swerve, before I even knew there was a vehicle coming out behind that hedge, a collision would have been certain.

I've had this experience more than once. I also remember slamming onto the brakes hard coming up to a green light at an intersection. My passenger then giving me a "what the hell are you doing" look, only to see, milliseconds later, another vehicle going full throttle through their red light.

You may have had similar experiences, too.

So where do these impulses come from? Although less dramatic, your day to day impulses from the state of alignment are one in the same. The sudden impulse to step into a coffee shop, where you end up meeting someone attractive who ends up asking you out on a date. The impulse to just go to your laptop and start writing or shooting a short video that ends up going viral and draws in new clients. The unexplainable impulse to walk down a specific aisle, only to find something you wanted that you hadn't realized was available.

These impulses, from life-saving maneuvers to being guided to your favorite candy in a candy shop, are coming from the greater part of you, the nonphysical, infinite intelligence source part of you that I like to call your inner being. You can call it the universe, God, nonphysical infinite intelligence, it's really all the same. It doesn't matter what you call it, but here's what's important.

> **Understand that the physical you, the you that you know exists here and now, isn't all of you. A larger part of you that you aren't aware of, still exists in the nonphysical.**

UNDERSTAND THE ROLE OF THE NONPHYSICAL YOU

This nonphysical part of you (let's call it your inner being), resides in the nonphysical. Like a parent free from having an inner critic or ego, it's unconditionally loving. It's always there for you, it has your back, is always supporting you and would never leave you or abandon you.

You have dreams and desires. So does your inner being. In fact, before you came into the physical, you came up with a game plan. You chose what themes you wanted to explore during your physical reality experience, including which parents (a.k.a. your physical reality entry point) or circumstances would be best suited to help you explore such themes.

Since you and your inner being are one and the same (two parts of the same thing), your dreams and desires are shared. Your ego may step in and trigger certain dreams and desires, but your authentic and most cherished dreams and desires are shared by both you and your inner being. These are the things you want the most at the core of your being.

You and your inner being both have different roles and responsibilities.

The role of the physical you is to experience physical reality in all its glory. You are the experiencer and your task is to experience the physical. To dream up your desires, follow your excitement, experience joy, daydream, and expand into new awareness through the circumstances that present themselves to you.

The role of the nonphysical you, your inner being, is to do the leg work. It's responsible for the creating. Because it resides in the timeless nonphysical place of infinite intelligence, it knows the path of least resistance to all your core and authentic desires. It has the ability to guide you to them, to create the magical synchronicities, to feed you the intuitive nudges to lead you down that path. But, only if you are listening – which can only happen when you're in alignment.

You didn't come here to figure it all out – your inner being already has that covered.

You didn't come here to solve problems – he/she's got that covered, too.

You didn't come here to effort – nope, your inner being can guide you around that.

You didn't come here to save anyone else – they have their own inner being for that.

You didn't come here to struggle – the only reason you do is because you are living life disconnected from your inner being.

> You and your inner being have a common goal. A common path that you set the intent to move down when you got here into the physical. This path is the path of greatest value, of greatest satisfaction, of greatest growth, of greatest pleasure, for both you and your inner being. This path is the absolute greatest path you can walk. It's called the path of least resistance and on it are all your greatest dreams and all your greatest desires, even the ones you don't know you have yet.

Your inner being never looks back. It's always looking forward and always guiding you down your path. The more you allow yourself to be in alignment, the more you allow yourself to be your authentic self without allowing fears to hold you back, the more easily you move down your path.

How does this all relate to action taking? Simple. The only action you ever need to worry about, the only action you ever need to take, is the action step your inner being is guiding you to do next. You don't know your path, but your inner being does. You don't know how to get from point A to point B, but your inner being does. You don't know the quickest and easiest way to your desires, but your inner being does.

The tricky part is that your inner being doesn't give you the entire map at once. In fact, it doesn't give you the map at all. It will only ever give you the next step, one step at a time. How do you know what your next step is along this path? Excitement.

FOLLOWING THE PATH OF HIGHEST EXCITEMENT

Excitement is THE highest form of intuition. Excitement is literally guidance from your inner being. In any given moment, your highest excitement is what your inner being is telling you to do next.

> **The only action step you EVER need to take is the one that feels best and excites you the most.**

That excitement isn't always going to be the most grandiose action step, but it's always going to be what you need to continue moving down your path. In any given moment, your highest excitement might be to visit a bookstore, it might be to take a vacation to Thailand, it might be to put an offer on a house or it might be to go take a nap.

Every single impulse of excitement, or what feels best in any given moment, is your next action step. From a practical standpoint, as a new paradigm experiencer of physical reality, the process of action-taking really does become that simple. What might get in your way of proper action-taking?

Rationality

In the old paradigm, you aren't aware of your inner being or the guidance it provides you. If you want to get from A to B, you come up with a plan, then you act on it because to your logical, rational mind, that's what makes sense.

In the old paradigm, following your excitement feels reckless and irresponsible. The old paradigm doesn't understand the importance of vibration. It doesn't understand that your inner being already has it all figured out and you just need to follow that path. Your inner being knows that guiding you into a specific bookstore may lead to a synchronistic encounter with someone who becomes your new business partner, and that propels you to a new level of success. Your old paradigm inner critic however, convinces you that going to a bookstore is a waste of time and that you need to stay at your desk and continue efforting and working hard.

Fear

Fear is also a big proponent of what holds you back from your path. Your inner being would never guide you into contrast that was non-serving or didn't have purpose behind it. It's always coming from the unconditionally loving place and knows what is best.

From the old paradigm vantage point, we're unaware of the existence of our path. We're unaware that we're infinite nonphysical beings having a human experience. We fear things going wrong. We fear taking action that will put us in a worse place than where we currently stand. I've worked with many clients who stay stuck in situations that are no longer serving them. Jobs that bring them safety and security, for example, but which are also no longer fun or exciting. Giving up what they are passionate about doing out of fear of not being successful. I see men and women who stay in relationships that no longer serve them, thinking that if they leave, they may not find something better than where they currently stand.

Your inner being would never lead you to a worse place than where you currently stand. There may be a transition period, with some discomfort and things to work through, but it is always ultimately guiding you to a better, more serving, and more satisfying place.

How else does fear hold us back? Let's look at fear of failure, for example, one of the fears most of my clients need to address. As humans we see failure as a bad thing. We see failure as, well, failure.

> ## If you aren't allowing yourself to fail, you aren't allowing yourself to succeed.

Every time the Wright brothers crashed a prototype plane before their first flight, was this a failure or a stepping stone to success?

Every startup I worked in that went under, before the big acquisition, were those failures or stepping stones to success?

Every past relationship that ended, that helped you bring a better understanding of who you are and what you want, were those failures or stepping stones to success?

If we want to be successful in life, we need to experience the thing we may not prefer, not because we came here to suffer, but because these are the experiences that lead to the necessary growth to align us with what we truly want – and our inner being knows that, which leads us to our next point, expectation.

Expectation

You may think you know, but you have no idea.

Occasionally I guide my kids into doing something they might not want to do. It's not because I'm mean or I feel the need to show my dominance as a father. It's because from that unconditionally loving place, I know that these things will serve them. It might teach them good habits, it might show them the importance of eating vegetables, or putting away their toys. They don't like it. Often times they might get mad at me because they don't understand the purpose behind it. As their father I have more awareness and a greater overall perspective which I know is in their benefit, even if they don't see it in those moments. One day, hopefully, they'll see and appreciate it as they grow older.

This same type of dynamic exists between you, your inner being and the guidance it provides. It has an all-seeing, grander perspective than we can ever imagine. It knows the path of least resistance, it knows the best possible place to guide us, and because we aren't always aware of the path, where it takes us or how a circumstance fits into the bigger picture, we hold ourselves back.

In your inner being's eye, it is not about a destination, it's about the process along the path to the destination that is important, because the process is what ultimately creates the transformation you need, at the vibrational level, that creates the shifts leading you further down your path.

By teaching my kids to clean their room each morning and make their beds, it's not about the end goal of having a made bed. It's about the confidence, respect and habits they learn in the process of making their bed each morning.

THE PROCESS IS THE POINT

As human beings we live our lives as end-goal-focused. Everyone, every day, is working on achieving something. An A+ in math. A promotion. The nicest landscaped yard on the block. Striving and reaching with a mindset akin to 'life isn't good enough' or 'I can't stop until this goal is met.'

Having strong desire is good, as long as it doesn't take you out of appreciation and satisfaction for where you currently stand – as long as you're not putting yourself in the energy of lack in retrospect to that desire. But this drive trips us up. We lose sight of what we really came here for – the process. We get so caught up in achieving that thing, we aren't benefiting from what our current circumstances, and the process of life itself, are trying to show us.

Why is it that the process, not the destination, is the important part?

Because when you understand that you are living in the new paradigm, where physical reality is driven by vibration, you understand that the physical reality experiences aren't what matter.

It's how you respond that matters.

> **It's the expansion and awareness you gain from these circumstances (the process) that matter because these are what create the vibrational shifts in you, and which ultimately bring you closer to the desires you really want.**

Let's break this down one more time.

There is what we believe we need, and there is what our inner being knows we need.

Old Paradigm thinking: This is the action step I need to take, based on what my rational mind is telling me, to get to my goal.

New Paradigm awareness: I don't know where my inner being is guiding me, or what the outcome will be, but that's okay because this process (regardless of its outcome) will bring me the awareness and vibrational shift I need to bring me closer to my goal.

One of the common fears many of my clients work through is the fear of failure, often led by expectation.

False expectations of what something should look like easily sway us from the path and true process of what our inner being is guiding us down. Sometimes failure, not getting what we want, is the process we need. By having expectations of what a circumstance should look like, we try and control its unfolding. Sometimes we walk away from the circumstance altogether and disallow the unfolding we were guided here for in the first place.

GETTING PRACTICAL WITH ACTION TAKING

Shifting from the old paradigm to being a new paradigm action taker isn't going to happen overnight. You may want to set a morning reminder and like any habit, it will take practice to get it right. I've been working on new paradigm action-taking for years, and even though old habits still bring me back to old effort-based action-taking on occasion, I'm getting better and better.

Fears, similar to the ones described earlier in this chapter, may also try to get in the way. Identifying and working through those fears will be a natural part of the process. Your inner critic may be persistent try to hold you back. The more you work through these fears, the easier it will be to take action from the new paradigm vantage point.

Step 1. Be detached from the outcome and remember that the process is the point.

Don't push against, but simply allow the unfolding of physical reality circumstances to take place. Use the contrast to self-reflect and be introspective as to what growth and new awareness the situations you find yourself in are meant to bring to light. Ask the question, What is this circumstance trying to show me about me, my belief systems, and my vibration? Trust that whatever way your inner being is guiding you, through excitement, is the best possible path for your growth and for the achievement of your desires even if your inner critic doesn't see it.

Step 2. Follow the path of what feels best or activates the highest excitement.

Remember, you don't need to solve anything and your inner being knows the best possible path for you. It's always guiding you down that path and all you need to do is practice listening and following that guidance. Remember, that guidance may not always be grandiose. Sometimes your highest excitement may be to take a nap, while other times it could be to go jump out of an airplane (with a parachute of course).

Having trouble feeling excitement about anything? Excitement on some days or around some topics may feel stronger than others. If you don't feel excitement, check in on what you're inspired to do and whatever option feels lightest, go with that one.

For example, you wake up in the morning, tired and groggy. Getting up and going to the gym may not be a very pleasant or exciting thought after an evening of line dancing and tequila shots. But what feels lightest? The thought of going to the gym knowing how good you will likely feel after getting your workout in? Or to stay in bed and skip today's exercise all together? Choose the option that feels lightest.

If you're suffering from a long-term lack of excitement, consider whether you have any fear of being excited. Does it feel unsafe in any way? Are there fears of being disappointed and hurt if you do follow excitement? These are common limiting perspectives that suppress the ability to experience excitement. If no fears seem to be present, focus on alignment, as alignment opens up that communication channel to receive guidance through excitement.

Step 3. Don't perceive failure as failure.

Failure is not an indication that you've done something wrong or gone down the wrong path. Follow your path of excitement and take it as far as you can take it, until you believe there is nowhere else to go, or your excitement is leading you somewhere else. Remember, failure is an inner-critic perception from the limited viewpoint of not understanding the higher vibrational purpose of our circumstances. Your inner being may weave you in and out of situations or circumstances. One day you may be inspired to write and finish the first thirty pages of a novel. The next day you may be inspired to go to the beach and do other things. The inspiration to write may only come back months later. Trust in the unfolding, and don't try to force how or what the inner-critic mind believes needs to play out.

CHAPTER KEY CONCEPT SUMMARY

- The first key component in inspired action-taking is alignment.

- The best action-taking is following the guided steps we receive from our inner being, who has a much broader perspective than we can have in the physical.

- Impulse, excitement, and intuition are all forms of guidance and direction we receive from our inner being, from that place of alignment.

- Solving problems, figuring things out, helping others, effort, and struggle are all being handled by your inner being. None of these are your responsibility.

- The only action step you need to take is whatever action feels the best or most exciting in any given moment in which you find yourself.

- Common blocks that prevent you from following the inspired actions provided by your inner being include rationality, fear, and expectation.

- Our focus in life is frequently reaching for destinations and goals, when in reality, the process of the unfolding of life is what is important. Circumstances don't matter; it's how we respond that matters, as this is what allows the positive vibrational shifts that lead us down our path.

- Be detached from outcomes. In any given moment do what feels best, brings the most excitement or feels the lightest. Don't perceive any particular outcome as failure.

ACCELERATION

11

HOW TO GET INTO THE MANIFESTATION FAST LANE

I f you're fairly new to the art of manifestation and like most people, you may be thinking to yourself that it's great to learn about alignment, vibration, allowing, and action. But, how do I get the genie out of the bottle so it can give me the stuff I want?

If "stuff" is what you came here for, then this chapter is for you because we're going to begin to explore just that. How do I get the stuff I want, or specifically, how do I speed up manifestation?

THE UNIVERSE DOESN'T PLAY FAVORITES

Recently, in one of my Facebook groups, after a bit of engagement, someone commented that I was a "master." Although I appreciate the compliment, it's important to understand that no one human being is any more of a master than anyone else. Not one person has an easier or more powerful ability to manifest.

Everyone is on the same level playing field.

Although everyone comes into physical reality with a different set of circumstances and possibly different vibrational intent, we all have the same ability to expand, grow, evolve and manifest.

The only difference between where you and anyone else stands is awareness and the vibration you practice.

The law of gravity doesn't treat anyone differently. It's consistent and applies to all things. The Law of Attraction is a law just like gravity and is equally consistent. It applies to each and every one of us in the exact same consistent way.

The universe, God, your inner being, or any other external source does not dictate what you can or cannot have. No outside force determines how easy or hard your life will be. At birth you're not assigned a high or low deservingness score looming in the shadows of your life experience.

Want it? You can have it.

Picture this. A loving mother, who has unconditional love for her four-year-old son, is walking through an outdoor market on a hot sunny afternoon. Out of the corner of her eye, she notices an ice cream stand with over fifty flavors. She walks over with her son, orders a double scoop of his favorite chocolate ice cream, then proceeds to sit down on a bench, and eat it all herself without sharing a single bite.

Would this scenario ever play out if the mother was truly unconditionally loving towards her son? Would any mother, who cared deeply for their child, wave something in their child's face that the child strongly desires but can not have?

Of course not, and your inner being wouldn't do this to you either.

Earlier in this book we talked about excitement. How excitement is one of the highest forms of inner guidance.

Excitement is fed to you from your inner being, pointing you in a direction, giving you your next action step.

Excitement is evidence that you can have it.

Being excited about something is evidence in itself that it is something you can have. Your inner being would never get you excited about something you can't have. It would never get you excited about anything that is out of your reach. The things you desire may look slightly different than how you perceive it should or will look like, but it will not be any less satisfying in any way.

You came here for the stuff. You didn't come to physical reality to escape from physical reality, you came here to indulge in all of it.

What do I mean by this? Some spiritual teachers teach that in order to find enlightenment, you need to detach from material things. Although I do agree that we do not want to allow ourselves to be dependent on stuff in order to find happiness, it is important to remember that we came here for the experience of the physical.

We are spiritual beings having a physical experience.

You don't buy chocolate chip ice cream just for the chocolate chips. You buy it for the entire experience – the chips, the ice cream and the cone. You didn't come to physical reality just to learn about topics such as unconditional love or forgiveness. You came here for all facets of the experience, and that experience includes physical reality stuff. From a spiritual or nonphysical standpoint there is no shame in desiring and indulging in the stuff. My only suggestion is, don't become dependent on it to achieve your desired emotional state. Your desires for all things, physical or nonphysical, are valid, and you shouldn't feel the need to justify them to anyone else.

UNDERSTANDING ACCELERATION

The fourth and final A, is Acceleration – the act of increasing speed or velocity – also frequently referred to in the world of manifestation as building momentum.

When you get into a vehicle, turn it on, take it out of park and into drive (before hitting the gas), your vehicle is in a standstill state. It waits until you hit the gas to move forward at the speed and acceleration based on how hard you push the pedal. You are the one who is responsible for the acceleration of the car towards its destination.

If your desire was represented by a car, it would behave a little differently.

Picture a sports car. A fast one. Maybe it's a Porsche, Ferrari, or a Tesla. For the remainder of this chapter this vehicle is going to represent one of your desires, any desire you'd like.

The moment your intent is set that you want a specific desire, the car is already in drive and the gas pedal is almost fully engaged. Your car is already in full acceleration towards your destination (manifestation of the desire). Momentum is inherent, meaning that once your intent is set, your desire is already on its way to you.

So then, why hasn't the desire you want shown up yet?

Because even though you've got the gas pedal fully engaged, you've got your other foot on the brake. Your brake is creating resistance slowing things down, maybe even bringing your car to a crawl. For virtually everyone, the key to increasing acceleration and momentum is not to press harder on the gas, but to take your foot off the brake.

Practically speaking, in what ways do I see people putting their foot on the brake?

- Split Energy – Fear of moving forward, fear of taking action, or fear of the consequences of having that desire.

- Negative Emotions – Especially the dominant ones, pulling you from alignment and preventing you from being a vibrational match to the desire.

- Impatience – Keeping you in the vibration and awareness of the absence (lack) of the desire.

- Desperation – Keeping you in lack energy, once again practicing the vibration of the absence of the desire.

- Stuck in a current reality loop – Constantly creating more of the same stuck-ness by observing more of the same current reality circumstances.

- Effort – Effort once again keeps you in the vibration of lack as you're continually pushing against what you don't want, which likely takes you out of alignment as well.

These are the gremlins, the things getting on peoples' backs that prevent success. Overcoming these is the bulk of the work you'll be looking at in your quest to manifestation, and we'll soon look at these in great detail. First, I want to take a look under the hood and talk about the mechanics of accelerating manifestation. I want to teach you what builds even more momentum before we start taking the foot off the brake.

EMOTIONAL INTENSITY – THE TURBO FUEL

Did you know that the Latin derivative of the word emotion, 'emotere,' literally means energy in motion? Think about that for a second.

Emotion. Energy in Motion.

When you are feeling emotions, you are literally putting energy in motion. What kind of energy? The energy that creates worlds, of course. The energy that leads to manifestation.

> **Anytime you are feeling emotion you are fueling your physical reality with the vibrational frequency of that emotion. The stronger, and more intensely you feel an emotion, the more motion you create and the more powerful the fuel.**

In the context of manifestation of specific desires, the more intensely you allow yourself to feel the positive emotions you experience when dreaming of the desire, the more momentum you are building towards it.

Keep in mind, in the case of negative emotions, you're creating fuel in the opposite direction hence slowing down the manifestation, creating more momentum towards lack or the unwanted experience.

What does this all mean from a practical standpoint? The fuel you put into your car is important. The higher the quality of the fuel you use, the better your car will perform. When it comes to the vehicle of manifestation, do you want to fill it with regular unleaded, or high-performance jet fuel? Both choices are always available and up to you. The greater intensity and more positive feeling state, the greater and more powerful the fuel.

FOCUS - SKIPPING THE SCENIC ROUTE

When I look back on my tech days playing in the world of startups, I met a lot of different people, many of whom were entrepreneurs. What I've noticed as key traits in those who are highly successful, are two specific things.

1. Laser Focus.

2. Strong Drive.

Most people who look at these successful entrepreneurs believe it's passion and hard work that drives success. Passion is part of it, because the passion is translated from excitement, an indicator that they are following guidance from their inner being in what they are pursuing. That's why passion leads to success. The hard work on the other hand, isn't what drives the success. There may be a strong belief *behind* the hard work which leads to success, but I believe the true driver is the laser focus.

If a complete stranger asked you to run to the grocery store to pick up some laundry detergent for them, which of the following two scenarios feels easiest?

Scenario one, they get specific. They tell you which brand, what size container, whether they want the powder or liquid format. You know exactly what they want.

Scenario two, they don't provide any detail. You arrive at the store, head to the right aisle and gaze upon the dozens and dozens of options to choose from, having no idea which one they prefer.

Is it easier for you to find and deliver the most pleasing option for them if they've gotten specific, or stayed more general?

Physical reality works the exact same way.

The more specific and detailed in the context of your desires, the greater the acceleration and more momentum generated towards it. When I know exactly what I want when looking at a shelf of products, it only takes a few seconds to grab what I'm looking for. When I'm uncertain, however, it will often take me a number of minutes to browse through all the options to determine which to put in my cart.

However, be cautious of the way you feel as you get specific and detailed. If getting specific creates fears, doubt, worry, negative emotions, take a step back and go back to

135

being more general until you can work through those sources of resistance.

PUTTING ACCELERATION INTO PRACTICE

The following three exercises are what I believe to be the best way to build more acceleration towards a desire.

Exercise 1 - Detailed intent setting

This exercise is also frequently referred to as pre-paving. In your mind, jump to a point in the future where your desire has already manifested. From that point, using a pen or pencil on paper (it has more of a vibrational imprint than using a keyboard or smartphone), write about your desire in present tense. Using present tense is crucial. Being in present tense puts you in the vibration and state of being where the desire is present now. If you practice the vibration of "when it will get here" or "it's on its way" the desire will be forever on its way.

It doesn't matter if you write as a stream of sentences or bullet points, use any format you want, but the key is to get as specific and detailed as possible. If you're writing about a relationship, for example, write about anything from hair color, to shoe size, to their job, hobbies, where they hang out, what they drive, etc. I also suggest using lots of emotions. Don't just talk about physical characteristics – get into emotions. How does that job or new relationship make you feel? Safe? Free? Loved? Again, get as detailed as possible.

Exercise 2 - Embodiment Mediation and Visualization

Embodiment is the second exercise I instruct my clients to do once they've completed pre-paving. Embodiment is the act of embodying the desire from a more emotional standpoint. Where the previous exercise of writing and getting detailed is more of a mental exercise, the embodiment meditation and visualization is more of an emotional exercise in which you practice tuning into the emotional states of your desire (filling your car with jet fuel). I have a guided visualization meditation specifically designed for this process available in the bonus companion content. Or, you can do the process yourself in silent meditation or listening to music you find boosts you into positive emotions. Spend those 15 minutes in dreamland, imagining the experience of your desired manifestation having come to fruition. Using all your senses, feel and boost your positive emotions as intensely as possible. Use all five senses. How does the desire feel, how does it smell? Experience the dream in the most vivid detail possible.

Exercise 3 - Segment Embodiment

The process of segment embodiment is picking out a segment of your day where you act as if, in your current physical reality, your desire is present. For example, if there is a certain car you're looking to manifest, when you drive your current vehicle, work on feeling as though (embodying) you're actually sitting in the car you want to be driving. Wanting to manifest a dream kitchen renovation? Before you get out of bed every morning, talk yourself into believing you're about to get out of bed and go make your coffee and breakfast in that kitchen.

The goal of segment embodiment is to make the desire feel as real as possible, as if it already exists and you are experiencing it. Homework I've assigned to relationship clients has involved asking their friend to order and send them flowers once or twice a month, with a card signed "from your boyfriend" or "from your girlfriend." Another favorite is to have them take the phone number that calls them the most and change the name in the address book to "my boyfriend" or "my girlfriend," so that every time this person calls you're momentarily in the energy of receiving a call from your significant other. Just don't accidentally answer with "Hey, honey" when the person on the other end might actually be your mom. These exercises don't have to involve someone else – it could be as simple as having an extra toothbrush on hand or making room in the closet for the relationship about to be manifested.

Exercise 4 - Speaking into Existence

Speaking into existence is just as it sounds. The difference between writing something into existence, and speaking it, is that you put the pen and paper aside and speak about the desire, out loud, as if it already exists. This can be awkward at first and take a bit of practice, but this process can be very powerful for some people. Many of my clients have also said that voicing the desire into the speech recorder on their phone made the process easier.

THE POWER OF APPRECIATION

When it comes to building acceleration and momentum towards a desire, I've saved the best for last. Appreciation.

Appreciation is slightly different than embodiment or intent setting, in that it's not specific to a particular desire. Appreciation is more of a general form of acceleration rather than driving towards something in a specific sense.

How does appreciation fit into our analogy using a sports car to represent manifestation? Highly charged positive emotional states are like going from regular to jet fuel. Getting detailed and specific directs you toward exactly where you want to go. Appreciation is what prevents you from having a child in your back seat who, every two minutes, keeps asking, "Are we there yet?"

Nothing, and I mean nothing, makes a trip from here to there feel any slower than the constant nagging voice of

"Are we there yet?" When both my kids are *game on*, it can literally make a ten- minute drive feel like ten hours. It feels like time is crawling to a near halt.

What's the opposite experience?

Having so much fun, enjoying life so much, you don't care how long it's going to take to get there because you're enjoying life and APPRECIATING the experience of your life, right where you're at.

Time flies when you're having fun. Time flies when you're in appreciation.

Learning to appreciate life, in an authentically non-forced way (because not everyone who says they practice appreciation are actually feeling appreciation – feeling, once again, is key) is going to get you where you want to go, and let in the things you want, much more quickly.

How do you practice and spend more time in the vibration of appreciation?

Dissatisfaction comes from a mindset of lack – it's the practice of noticing what you have not yet achieved or noticing what you do not have. Satisfaction, (a benchmark of appreciation – I see them as going hand in hand), is the practice of noticing the positive things you do have, and how far you've come.

What's the difference between someone who dominantly practices appreciation versus someone who doesn't?

Habit.

Have you ever noticed seeing someone working in the customer service industry, maybe at a local coffee shop or grocery store, who is always in a bad mood and complaining? Alternatively, have you ever noticed that some people are always in a good and positive mood? Have you ever considered what makes someone consistently unpleasant or consistently in a good mood? Is it just a character trait they're born with? *Of course not.* It's a pattern of behavior they've developed over time, most frequently from an influential figure like a parent or sibling in their life.

How do you develop more appreciation, which leads to acceleration? The same way you develop any new habit. Practice it. How do you stop smoking? Decide to throw your smokes out. How do you stop eating junk food? Stop buying it. How do you stop talking negatively about others? Stop doing it. How do you stop practicing dissatisfaction and reach for the other end of the spectrum? Consciously practice new thought patterns, develop new neuropathways which, over time, will become a habit. Can't find anything to appreciate?

If you knew that oxygen could run out at any minute, would you appreciate the oxygen you're breathing in right now? If you knew that none of your neighbors had access to clean drinking water, would your perspective on the water you have access to in this moment change? These may be overly simplistic examples, but they help demonstrate the nature of appreciation and how the state of appreciation is driven by perception.

GET PRACTICAL WITH APPRECIATION AND JOURNALING

Attitude of Gratitude is a common statement in the world of self help, and gratitude journaling is the very first thing that comes to mind for virtually everyone.

I'm not downplaying journaling, I encourage it, but keep in mind, there is a subtle, yet significant difference between appreciation and gratitude.

I am grateful for the food on my plate.

I appreciate the food on my plate.

Take a moment and see if you can feel the energy in both of these statements. Which statement feels lighter to you? The difference is very subtle, which some people can't tell, but here's what's important.

In gratitude, there is often a vibration of lack or absence.

In the statement, 'I am grateful for the food on my plate,' there is an underlying imposition of the possibility of not having food on my plate. A very minute, but still present, hint of the vibration of lack.

Appreciation, however, is more purely focused on the presence and satisfaction of that thing on which you are focused.

Gratitude isn't bad, it's great to be grateful, but in the context of vibration and manifestation, appreciation is just one step up.

Appreciation Journaling can be done anytime during the day, but I suggest first thing in the morning, as it will help set the tone for the rest of the day. The important part is to do your journaling with a pen or pencil on paper, as it creates more of a vibrational imprint. You feel those statements more. The universe doesn't care what you say. It doesn't even care what you write down on paper. What it responds to is the vibration you're putting out, and how you feel is the indication of that vibration. In a nutshell, what you feel as you are in the process of journaling is most important.

Start with just five things. If it flows, reach for ten. Can you make it all the way to twenty? Thirty? How far can you go? Even if you write the same thing down over and over again, even if you can only find just one thing to tune into that creates that deep feeling of appreciation, that's all it takes. Just one thought, just one seed to trigger the feeling. You can keep going back to it as much as you'd like. The greater the feeling, the more energy you are putting in motion.

SEGMENT APPRECIATING

Journaling isn't for everyone, and to be honest, it's great to get into the vibration of appreciation once or twice a day, but in order to create a habit of appreciation you want to integrate the practice of appreciating into the various segments of your day.

A desire that's been at the top of my list for a few years is a second home closer to where my kids stay with their mom. The back-and-forth drive is about two hours each way from my coastal home here in New Brunswick to their mom's house in the central part of the province. A second home would be more convenient and give me the opportunity to spend even more time with my kids.

When making the drive between the two locations, I alternate between listening to my favorite teachers and podcasts and putting on good upbeat music that pumps me up. This is when I like to do my appreciation work. I observe the beautiful trees in the fall, I appreciate the bald eagles along the roads that weave along the Saint John River. I think about my kids, my relationship, the work I do, my amazing clients. This is my alone time to practice appreciating when I have no distractions other than the occasional pothole to be avoided.

As your day plays out, choose segments of it where you intend to practice being in appreciation during that time. It could be the thirty minutes you spend cleaning the house, or folding laundry. It could be the hour you spend weeding the garden or the twenty-minute break between tasks at work. The when doesn't matter, but if you can take just ten to twenty minutes over the course of the day, three to five times, you'll begin to strengthen your appreciation muscle. Over time you'll notice you start doing it more naturally, you'll cross a threshold and it'll become your new default.

PUTTING IT ALL TOGETHER

We've explored a number of different approaches and exercises that will lead to greater acceleration toward desires in this chapter. Don't let it overwhelm you. You don't need to do it all or figure it all out at once. Start with whichever of these exercises or approaches feels easiest for you to implement. Practice it long enough for it to become easy and natural before adding on another. Take it one step at a time – this work is a marathon, not a race. You may not see the results you're looking for right away; real and lasting change doesn't typically happen overnight. Enjoy the process, have fun with it, and eventually you'll begin to notice the rewards of your practice experiencing a much quicker and smoother ride in your manifestation sports car, without the kids screaming in the backseat.

CHAPTER KEY CONCEPT SUMMARY

- Everyone is on the same level playing field – no one person has a stronger ability to manifest than another. Awareness and the concepts taught in this book are the only differentiators between one person's ability to manifest and another's.

- Your inner being would never get you excited about a desire that you can't have.

- Your desires inherently accelerate towards you the moment your intent is set. The key is not to push harder on the gas, but to take your foot off the brake that slows it down from making its way to you.

- Negative emotions, split energy, impatience, desperation, stuck and effort are all means by which we put our foot on the brake.

- Laser focus, appreciation journaling, as well as strong positive emotional intensity, will all create positive momentum toward desire.

WEALTH, HEALTH, AND RELATIONSHIPS

12

A GUIDE TO MANIFESTING LOVE AND RELATIONSHIPS

M anifesting your dream relationship is the first of what I call the big three. The big three are the things in the world of manifestation which men and women desire to attract the most. They consist of love, money, and health, and we'll be addressing each of these in the chapters that follow.

Even if you already have the perfect lover, all the money you could ever desire or great health, I don't suggest skipping these chapters, as they may provide valuable insight into aspects you may not consider or elements you may have going on in your vibration.

When it comes to The Law of Attraction, there is nothing more telling about what we have going on in our vibration than relationship circumstances and the partners we attract.

Take Lara, for example.

Lara is a tall beautiful, intelligent woman in her mid-thirties who lived in the United States, someone whom I had met early in my coaching practice. A friend who had seen one of my videos suggested she reach out to me, which she did.

Lara struggled with relationships as long as she could remember. Almost in tears, she explained to me that over the last fifteen to twenty years, since her senior year of high school to be precise, no relationship ever lasted more than three months. Her friends were mostly married, already having children, and she felt as though time was running out. Fed up, feeling hopeless and frustrated, she just couldn't understand what was wrong, no longer knew what to do, and was succumbing to the belief that it was time to give up and accept her role as a crazy cat lady.

I quickly reassured her that we could easily identify and resolve the root cause, as I instinctively knew that she was likely suffering from split energy. I asked Lara to recollect her first significant relationship. She shared that it was the only relationship that ever lasted more than three months, her first, back in high school.

Lara was dating one of her classmates. She fell in love, and after a number of months decided he was her Prince Charming, and that they were soulmates. In her mind they were going to get married, have babies (she already had names picked out), and live happily ever after.

Unfortunately for Lara, things didn't work out as planned. One morning as she arrived at school, she found out that he had been cheating on her. The unexpected news caught Lara off guard, and this emotionally crushing and traumatic experience has impacted her relationships and ability to attract love ever since.

One of the roles of your subconscious mind is to keep you safe. Like a virus scanner on a computer, it's always analyzing and monitoring your experiences to ensure they won't bring you any harm. As this was Lara's first significant relationship, her first time falling in love, with the end result of being hurt and emotionally traumatized, her subconscious mind deemed relationships and falling in love as unsafe.

From this moment on, anytime Lara would get close to someone she was dating and start to fall in love, subconscious fears would sneak in resulting in self-sabotage. Around the two-to three-month mark, she would start causing fights or initiate other behavior that would result in the relationship falling apart. She noticed the pattern, but never realized she was the initiator, let alone understanding why she was doing it. Lara was suffering from split energy.

> **Split energy is when part of us wants something, but another part of us – often subconscious, is afraid of it.**

In Lara's case, part of her wants to get married, have babies and live happily ever after with that special someone. But her subconscious fears relationships because the consequences can be emotionally traumatic as she experienced in high school.

Split energy can show up in various forms and the root cause doesn't always need to be as traumatic. It's also a very common occurrence. I would estimate that roughly seventy-five to eighty percent of women suffer from split energy due to negative past relationship circumstances or unhealthy behavior witnessed between their parents growing up.

Here are just three common fears in the context of relationships resulting in split energy.

The fear of being controlled – typically rooted in having experienced a relationship with a partner who was possessive, jealous, or controlling.

The fear of being cheated on – typically rooted in having been cheated on or witnessing infidelity between your parents.

The fear of being hurt (physically or emotionally) – typically rooted in having experienced a past relationship involving traumatic breakups or an abusive partner.

How do you know if you suffer from split energy? Ask yourself the following question and see what answer comes to mind. "If I meet that special someone tomorrow, and things start to get serious and we start to fall in love, how does that feel unsafe? What's the worse thing that could happen?"

If these questions surface any fears, you'll want to explore and work on clearing them to resolve the split energy.

A second impact of split energy is not being able to attract a partner at all. If you've been single for a long time and struggle to attract anyone, even for a date, you likely also suffer from split energy.

When a greater part of us feels as though relationships are unsafe, we vibrationally put up a wall or barrier – maybe we should call it a relationship forcefield. At a subconscious level we are always putting out, and tuning into, the vibes of others. Vibrationally speaking, if you're putting out vibes of "I'm afraid to be in a relationship and part of me doesn't want a relationship, as it's risky," potential partners, even when attracted to you, are picking up on that vibe. The end result is that you won't get approached at all.

This is what I often call being comfortably single.

In the context of relationships, split energy is only one of the two key aspects you want to look at. The second, of course, is emotions.

Split energy is what defines the ease of attraction. When present, it's what makes attracting and staying in a relationship challenging.

Emotions (and the perspectives behind them) are the second key aspect that need to be explored, as they define the types of partners you attract and relationship circumstances you find yourself in.

If your attraction point contains strong dominant negative emotions of abandonment, for example, you'll likely attract partners who are emotionally unavailable or who have a tendency to abandon you.

If your attraction point contains the feelings of being stuck and powerless, you'll likely attract partners who are controlling, manipulative, jealous and possibly narcissistic.

If your attraction point contains the emotion of not good enough, then your partner may treat you poorly and seem impossible to please, or even cheat on you.

THE FIVE ARCHETYPES OF ATTRACTION

In my previous book, a short kindle ebook called <u>Single No More</u>, I've categorized these patterns of attraction into five basic archetypes. I call these the archetypes of attraction, and they model the types of relationships we attract based on the emotional baggage we carry. Most men and women I've worked with match one to three of these archetypes. Some will have one strong dominant match, while others will be split between a few. On occasion someone will match all five.

Everyone has a unique fingerprint of life experiences, hence a unique mix of emotions in their attraction point. If you match one (or many) of these archetypes, it doesn't mean this will be your pattern for the rest of your life. The goal of my defining these archetypes is to bring you the awareness of what emotions you may be carrying that are responsible for the relationship circumstances in which you find yourself. If you identify with an archetype, investigate these emotions for yourself, and by shifting these from your attraction point, you'll no longer match the archetype, and the people you attract in relationships will change.

Below is a list of all five archetypes along with a short description of each. In the bonus companion content, you'll find a webinar recording where I review all five archetypes and take listeners through a process to help identify yours. This process may not be necessary, however, as you might recognize right away which archetypes you match.

1 - THE VICTIM (POWERLESS)

Individuals who match The Victim archetype often attract partners who are controlling, dominating or who don't listen and give you a sense you're never being heard. They may be emotionally and/or physically abusive, manipulative, and need to control all the shots (passively using guilt or being directly aggressive). These partners can also be highly reliant on you in various ways. It could be that they lack responsibility in their own life, maintain a dependency on you to lift them up and be happy or have a need to be taken care of financially, for example.

Those who fall under The Victim archetype are carrying strong emotions reflecting a lack of control and powerlessness, driving an overall theme that you can't do what you want when in a relationship. Relationships may also feel unsafe over the fear of having a lack of control and freedom. If you find yourself being a match to The Victim archetype, you likely also suffer from poor personal boundaries, don't feel safe speaking up, and allow yourself to be easily taken advantage of. Growing up you may have had childhood circumstances where you were bullied, where you had a highly criticizing, controlling or judgemental parent, or were a victim of circumstances where you felt there was no way out.

Other circumstances that often match this vibration include money problems (lack of finances) and chronic lower back issues.

2 - THE UNWORTHY (NOT GOOD ENOUGH)

Individuals who match The Unworthy attract partners who seem unforgiving and are often displeased. No matter what you do or how hard you try, they are never satisfied and aren't afraid to drop the blame on you. These partners can often have bi-polar tendencies and it can be difficult to know how they will respond to various circumstances. No matter how hard you try or what you do, there is a general tendency that you aren't good enough. The Unworthy archetype is also a match to individuals who frequently attract partners with fidelity issues.

If this sounds like the partners you attract, you're likely a match to The Unworthy archetype and are likely carrying strong emotions of feeling unworthy or not good enough. Did you grow up feeling as though no matter how hard you tried or how well you did, it was never good enough? Did you lack praise from your parents, did they push you hard to do better, or were never satisfied with your accomplishments? Do you have perfectionist tendencies, or were you bullied in school? These are all traits common for The Unworthy archetype.

Individuals who carry these emotions suffer from chronic neck and shoulder pain or stiffness. If your partner was bi-polar and an overall sense of lack of safety was present in the relationship, you may also suffer from stomach and digestive issues such as Irritable Bowel Syndrome (IBS), frequently suffer from anxiety, or operate in states of fight or flight. This comes from the constant worry or threat (at a subconscious level) of a not being safe from the potentially negative verbal attack from a displeased partner.

3 - THE UNLOVEABLE (ABANDONMENT)

A third common archetype is The Unloved. Men and women who match this archetype attract partners who are often mentally and/or emotionally unavailable. These partners have a tendency to make you feel as though they don't support you. They often put other aspects of their life at a higher priority than their relationship with you. These partners may be workaholics, for instance, or people who prefer spending time with their friends than with you. Intimacy issues can also frequently surface with The Unloved archetype.

Men and women who are a match to The Unloved often carry emotions around abandonment, rejection, loneliness, lack of support and belief of not being loved or loveable. Childhood circumstances around having a parent who wasn't physically or emotionally present, such as the lack of a father figure, or parent who made you feel abandoned, is a common trait of individuals who match this archetype. Many of the women I've worked with who are still single later in life often match this archetype.

4 - THE RESCUER

The Rescuer archetype will find themselves in relationships where partners who struggle or need saving. These are often individuals who suffer from drug or alcohol addiction. It can also be individuals who suffer from mental health issues such as severe anxiety or depression. The rescuer often finds themselves in the caretaker role, spending a great deal of energy helping or trying to save or rescue their partner.

Those who match this archetype have often grown up in family situations where they may have had to step up and become the parent, even though they were the child. They may have been the responsible one in the family or the oldest sibling who took care of others. They've grown up feeling responsible for those around them and everyone else needs to come first, before their own well-being. They may also associate love or feeling loved by how much they do for others and the appreciation or praise they receive.

5 - THE COMFORTABLY SINGLE

The final archetype is different than other archetypes as it doesn't match any specific relationship pattern because relationships simply aren't present. The lack of relationship isn't because partners aren't available but because part of them doesn't want to be in a relationship. They are comfortably single. Although desiring to remain single isn't necessarily a problem, deep down, many of the individuals who match this archetype do want a relationship, even if they don't want to admit it to themselves.

The root cause of this archetype is often due to split energy.

ADDITIONAL KEY POINTS

Beyond the exploration of emotions in your attraction point and split energy, there are two other key points I always make (and explore) with my relationship clients.

1. Get clear on what you want

Another important step in partner attraction is of course, getting clear on what you want. Shortly before Anik and I met she shared that she made a bulleted list of details she wanted in her next partner. Of the fifty items on her list, I matched nearly all of them. Don't be afraid to get detailed and specific, using both physical as well as emotional attributes. Talk about how that person looks, how they make you feel, how you spend your time together, what they do for work, etc.

2. Explore The relationship between you and you

I'm sure you've heard it more than once, but it's too important to leave out – the most important relationship is the relationship between you, and you. Since you can't break up with yourself, it is the most important relationship you'll ever have. If you are serious about attracting a partner who falls madly in love with you, you want to be madly in love with yourself.

> **The more you accept yourself, the more you will attract a partner who accepts you. The more you unconditionally love yourself, the more you will attract a partner who will do the same. The more beauty you see in yourself, the more beauty your partner will see in you.**

Remember, what you are perceiving is always being reflected to you from physical reality, including how you perceive yourself. The more you allow yourself to be the authentic you, the more you are putting out your authentic vibration, resulting in a partner who will be drawn to your authentic vibration.

How does that translate?

The more you clear those negative emotions and perceptions that prevent you from loving yourself and being yourself, the more ideal of a partner you'll attract, matching who you truly are and what you truly want in a loving relationship.

CHAPTER KEY CONCEPT SUMMARY

- Relationships are one of the most telling life experiences that can bring us awareness of what we have going on in our vibration.

- In the context of relationships, we want to explore both the negative emotions we carry, as well as split energy.

- The emotions we carry define the type of partners and experience we attract in relationships.

- Split energy is responsible for self-sabotaging behavior, as well as keeping you single for extended periods of time.

- Exploring the archetypes of attraction will help you better understand your patterns and root causes so you can shift them and find yourself attracting better circumstances.

- As cliché as it sounds, the most important relationship is the one between you, and you.

13

HOW TO ALLOW THE LOVER TO SHOW UP

N ow that you know what you need to look at in the context of relationships, let's put it all together into clear and concise action steps so you can allow your way into the relationship you truly want.

IDENTIFY AND DEAL WITH SPLIT ENERGY

Of all the aspects you need to look at in the context of attracting love and relationships, split energy seems to be the one that stands out the most. Split energy can be rooted in anything from unexpected breakups and relationship traumas, to observing unhealthy dynamics in your parent's relationship as a kid.

Use the following digging questions to identify any split energy you may be carrying.

1. If I met someone, and over the next few months started to fall in love and get closer to that person, how does this feel unsafe?

2. If I met someone, and the relationship begins to develop into a long-term serious relationship, what's the worst thing that could happen?

If the answers to these questions pop into your head, then these fears are your sources of split energy. Work through these fears using the processes taught in this book or seek out the help of a well-trained practitioner.

If no answers come to mind, then there's a likely chance you don't have any split energy to deal with.

IDENTIFY AND DEAL WITH EMOTIONAL ROOT CAUSES (EXPLORE YOUR ARCHETYPES)

If you find yourself encountering the same unwanted circumstances over and over again in the partners you attract, you'll want to look at the emotional root causes. These are the emotions sitting in your attraction point allowing reality to reflect them back to you through your relationships.

Identify these emotions by looking at the dominant emotion that is triggered by current and past relationships. The archetypes from the previous chapter should also assist you in narrowing down these emotions if they aren't obvious to you.

Once identified, use the clearing processes outlined in this book or seek out the help from a well- trained practitioner.

GET CLEAR ON WHAT YOU WANT

The exercise I suggest to all my relationship clients is to create a relationship avatar. Using a pen or pencil on paper (I always prefer doing these exercises on paper as it has a more significant vibrational imprint), mentally jump to a certain point in the future, specifically, to the point at which the relationship has already been manifested. Speak about the relationship and that person in present tense, using as much detail as possible.

Speak about the following attributes:

- Their physical appearance.

- How they make you feel (emotions).

- What they do for work, how they spend their free time, including their hobbies.

- What the two of you do when together.

- Their background, where they are from, how much you get along and connect.

Remember, the more detail you provide, the greater the momentum you will create. You only need to do this exercise once, and there is no need to review. You can always come back and add more, make changes, or even redo this exercise if you feel inspired.

Once this exercise is completed, your intent is set, your order is placed, and your desire is on its way.

EMBODY THE RELATIONSHIP

Now that your order is set, your next step is to embody the relationship as if it already exists. Here are some embodiment exercises I frequently assign to those who are looking to manifest a new relationship.

- The Desire Embodiment Meditation. This meditation is a fifteen-minute guided meditation that will take you through an embodiment process that involves visualization and tapping into the emotional setpoints of your desire. This meditation is accessible in the bonus companion content.

- Get ready to be ready. If you knew this person was going to show up tomorrow, what would you do?

Would you get your hair done? Would you shave? Would you buy a new wardrobe, clean your house, or make room in the closet? Do all the things in anticipation of this person, from the energy of their already being here.

- A third and favorite exercise is to make the person real. Arrange for a friend to surprise you with a flower delivery once or twice a month, signed with a card from "my boyfriend" or "my girlfriend." Who is your most frequent caller on your phone? Change their name in your address book, so that when the phone rings, you see the words "my boyfriend" or "my girlfriend." These are all simple and fun techniques to help convince your mind and put you in the energy of this person being present in your life.

DATE YOURSELF

The most important of all relationships is the relationship between you and you. The more you love, appreciate, care for, and see the value in yourself, the more the person you attract will reflect the same. Dating yourself could feel awkward at first, but with some practice it gets easier. You might even begin to enjoy it.

What are some ways you can begin to date yourself?

- Treat yourself to dinner and a night at the movies.

- Pay yourself some compliments a few times a day.

- Spoil yourself with trips to the spa or a massage.

- Give yourself some "me time" away from kids, work, the daily grind of life.

- Take a vacation, following your passion and excitement, do what feels good, and be unapologetic.

These exercises won't only help you be in the vibration of being cared for and loved, they will help boost you into conducive states of alignment that are ripe for manifestation.

GET INTO ALIGNMENT, ALLOW AND STAY OUT OF EFFORT

For most people who struggle to manifest any strong desire, this step is often the hardest. In order to line up with your ultimate relationship, you want your inner being and the mechanism of synchronicity to do the work.

What does that mean?

You need to get out of the way. You need to take a step back, get off Tinder (unless that feels like an inspired action), and let your inner being do its work. A good exercise for allowing this process is through the use of a ritual or avatar where you hand off the responsibility to your inner being.

Your next step is to get out and have as much fun, and enjoy life as much as you possibly can until that relationship finds you. How do you know you're successful at this exercise? You're not busy looking or wondering when it's going to show up. You want to be enjoying life so much, you're not noticing its absence and that is when your desire will most likely appear.

ABOUT MANIFESTING YOUR EX BACK

Often times I'll run into someone who is desperately trying to manifest an ex back, such as Tom.

Tom was a tech guy from the Midwest, living in Silicon Valley. A super-successful, very intelligent, career-driven man. He reached out to me for help after watching one of my YouTube videos. He had no trouble attracting dates, but could never develop any interest to go beyond the very first one. No matter how smart, how attractive, how fun that person was, it was never enough.

Why? Because he just couldn't get over his ex, someone he had left over three years prior.

He knew logically that his ex wasn't good for him, that he could never have a lasting, healthy relationship with her. He was the one who ended the relationship, yet he still just couldn't get her out of his mind, even three years later.

> **Like most people, including those seeking to manifest an ex back, what Tom didn't realize is that it wasn't his ex that he was infatuated with, it was the way his ex made him feel.**

Oftentimes, when we experience the best relationship we've ever had, we tap into a unique feeling we've never experienced before. In Tom's case, it was a sense of feeling whole and complete; something he had never felt in his entire life, not even from his parents. Subconsciously Tom wasn't aware that she was making him feel this specific way; he just knew that she made him feel something he had never felt with anyone else.

The mistake Tom made, as do many others who are obsessed about someone from a past relationship, was believing this person was the only one who could make them feel this way.

Think of your favorite food from your favorite restaurant. Maybe it's the pizza joint down the street or the tiramisu at a restaurant in Italy or Mallorca. How do you know that it's the best ever? Just because it's the best you've had so far, does it automatically mean that there isn't a better slice somewhere else?

Just because you haven't had that better slice, does it mean it doesn't exist? No.

This same analogy applies to relationships as well. Just because a relationship was the best you've ever had, does not mean that person is the only one who can make you feel this same way—they're simply the first to have done so.

In Tom's case, we cleared the emotions of feeling incomplete and un-whole, which led to the obsession on the past relationship (soothing those two emotional voids). Without the emotional association to the ex and these emotions, he was no longer anchored to her, and his dating experiences immediately changed.

For all those chasing after a specific person such as an ex, I remind them this narrow-minded false belief is closing the door to all other potential relationships, including ones that can be even more satisfying. How can you truly know that your pizza joint is the best pizza joint in the entire country if you haven't tried them all? You can't. The same goes for relationships too.

CHAPTER KEY CONCEPT SUMMARY

- Identify and deal with sources of split energy.

- Identify and deal with negative emotions responsible for the archetypes you match.

- Get clear on what you want in a relationship and get specific about the attributes of the person you want to manifest.

- Embody the relationship to become a vibrational match to it.

- Date yourself.

- Get into alignment and stay out of effort.

- In the context of relationships, we want to explore both the negative emotions we carry as well as split energy.

14

A GUIDE TO MANIFESTING MONEY

I f you're not after a relationship, then there's a good chance you've come to this book looking to manifest money.

Money's a funny thing. I've worked with millionaire clients looking to reach billionaire status. I've personally manifested and seen others manifest seven-figure sums. I've seen others struggle to make ends meet, not sure where they'd be living at the end of the month. I've even received a personal video message from someone asking for $5000 so they could comfortably quit their day job in order to work with others.

For some people, manifesting money is as easy as breathing oxygen. For others, it's not.

One of my clients even manifested a sum of money equivalent to $1.3 million from a one-dollar investment during the housing market crash in the early 2000s. That's a 1,000,000x return on investment.

When you truly understand the law of attraction and the vibrational nature of reality, anything is possible, and that doesn't exclude the topic of money.

Everyone has the same potential when it comes to money and finances. No one person is more or less deserving. No one person needs to work harder than another. Money, like anything else, is all about the beliefs you hold and the vibration you practice.

People think that money is the key to their desires. The key to having everything you want. The paradox, however, is that for most people, money is doing the opposite. It's preventing desire and manifestation.

Let me explain. If you are a vibrational match to driving a luxury car, you'll experience that. If you're a vibrational match to being evicted, no amount of money can prevent it. If you're a vibrational match to yoga training in Bali, you'll manifest it. If you're a vibrational match to flying there in first class, you'll experience that too. If you're a vibrational match to driving an unreliable car, money can't get you around that either.

> *Money is not the enabler of experiences – your vibration is.*

What does this mean exactly? That in the context of the Law of Attraction, manifestation, and the physical reality experience, *money doesn't matter, only your vibration matters.*

Imagine this.

You came into physical reality with intent, with a plan. You've got a path. Your inner being is guiding you down that path, the path that many teachers call the path of least resistance. Your inner being never looks backwards, only forward towards the next step down your path, and it's always attempting to guide you there.

Now let's say the next step along your path is a specific training in Maui. Do you believe that your inner being would ever prevent you from moving down that path, due to lack of finances? "Sorry Bob, I guess you're out of luck, you don't have enough money to keep moving down your path of expansion and evolution."

Of course not.

Your inner being has the know-how and power to allow any desire, big or small, to present itself to you in whatever form is the least resistant. Money can never prevent you from an experience, it can never prevent you from moving down a path. Only the perception around the need of money can hold you back. If the need for money is required for a specific desire or experience, and you are a vibrational match to that desire or experience, the money has to show up. It must because anything you are a vibrational match to, you must experience. It's the law.

It may sound funny that in a chapter about money manifestation I'm telling you that you don't need money, but that's not the case. I don't want to discourage you from manifesting money. By all means, set your intent to claim the infinite abundance of wealth you deserve. The goal here is to simply allow you to gain the awareness that lack of money isn't holding you back – your vibrational state is. If you're like most people, money is acting as a limiting belief system that prevents you from moving forward in allowing desires to show up because you believe you need to figure out the money and have it show up first, before you allow yourself to create momentum towards a desire.

That's why for most people, money *prevents* manifestation, rather than enabling it. You're so busy or concerned about making the money show up, you're not creating momentum and energy towards the desire itself.

GIVE MONEY REASON TO MANIFEST

In my experience in the world of money manifestation, money tends to manifest much more easily when we give it a reason to manifest. It's like our inner being or physical reality gives us the money when we need it.

Take the example I used in the opening chapter, when I manifested the exact amount of money I needed, $18,000, for the down payment for my desired vehicle. The money didn't show up two weeks or a month earlier. It didn't show up late. The exact amount I needed arrived exactly when I needed it.

When I reflect back on clients who've manifested specific sums of money, I see this type of experience over and over again. Manifesting not a specific dollar amount, and then deciding what to do with the money, but giving your inner being a concrete and specific reason and need for those funds. Oftentimes, the amount manifested for that desire or experience is the exact amount needed.

If your highest excitement was to spend a year traveling the world for example, and you decided that you needed a budget of $500,000, what would be your first step?

For most people, that first step is finding a way for the money to show up. What kind of job do I need? How do I save up the funds? How do I make the money show up? Most people don't dive into the planning phase of the travel because they don't believe it's possible for them, without the money. So, why bother?

In reality, however, if manifesting the travel is your goal, you need to approach the manifestation from the flip side of the coin. Don't worry about the how – leave that up to your inner being. In the meantime, plan the travel in the greatest level of detail as possible. Choose flights, select your destination, speak to your travel partner. Get the energy and momentum flowing towards that desire and take it as far as you can possibly take it, with the understanding that the funds will make themselves present when needed. Practice the knowingness and vibration that you'll have what you need when you need it. If you can do this from a non-resistant place, if the funds are the last step and part of the path of least resistance, they will show up.

FREEDOM IS THE VIBRATION OF MONEY

Every physical reality desire we chase is rooted in how we believe we'll feel in the having of that desire. You may want a relationship to feel loved, connected, complete. You may want a certain promotion to feel successful, a sense of achievement, or good enough.

Why do we want money? There are two very specific beliefs rooted behind the desire of manifesting money.

One, which we've already addressed, is that we see it as the bridge to everything else we want. You should now know that money isn't the bridge – your vibrational state is.

Second, we believe money is freedom.

> **The dominant negative emotion behind the energy of lack of money, is stuckness. How do you feel when you can't figure out how to pay your bills, how to quit your job, how to afford the things you desperately want? You feel stuck.**

What's the perspective behind feeling stuck (remember, the emotion is the indicator of a negative false perspective that holds you back)? The false perspective is "I can't do what I want."

What's the best way for the mirror of physical reality to reflect back to you the belief or perspective that you can't do what you want? Lack of money.

Anytime someone brings up the topic of manifesting money, I always bring up three key points.

1. Focus on alignment and the vibration of the desire you would use the money for, not money itself.

2. Shift out of the energy and vibration of being stuck and move your way into a dominant feeling of freedom.

3. Stop working your way out of debt or lack, and instead, work your way into wealth.

We've already covered point number 1.

For key point number two, you need to shift from stuck to free. One end of the stick, to the other. But when we can't figure out how to get from point A to point B, how do we stop feeling stuck? By understanding why we feel stuck in the first place, and why the perspective behind it is wrong.

A number of years ago Calvin got in touch with me to help him work through some personal issues. He was in his thirties, felt as though he was in a rut; he was not happy with life or the direction it was taking, and he wasn't sure where to go or what to do. He was finishing up a college marketing degree that didn't excite him, some of his friends were bad influences, and drug use was starting to become an issue. He knew something had to change, and he didn't know what.

Near the end of one of our sessions, I remember asking Calvin what excited him. If he could do anything he wanted in life, what would it be? He shared with me that some of the best times in his life were when he took a motorcycle and traveled from Banff to Costa Rica, filming the entire trip. During this 35,000km adventure, he got on camera his experiences surfing and rock climbing, among other extreme adventures.

He shared with me that if he could do anything in the world, it would be traveling and filming adventure sports. But, he quickly added, the formal training needed to become a professional filmographer would be in the tens of thousands of dollars, let alone the cost of gear, and the scarcity of these types of gigs.

His conscious rational mind had convinced him this type of work was in the realm of impossibility for him. The thought of living out this dream made him feel stuck.

I gave Calvin some exercises, we did some belief work, and I sent him on his way.

Where is Calvin now?

Just a few years later, he now owns his own video production company. He's filmed professional ice climbers in China (including one climber he remembered idolizing in his early twenties), he's filmed big game hunting in Argentina, he's filmed extreme kayakers in the white waters of British Columbia.

How did he get there?

A Canadian camping company ran a national contest where the first prize was camping gear and a trip across Canada. Part of the submission was a video. Calvin ended up being one of the finalists for the contest. Although he didn't win, he was interviewed by the Canadian Broadcast Channel (CBC) radio network. They were so impressed by his video and subsequent interview, they offered him a contract to work for them as an adventure columnist.

This contract ballooned into opportunities involving media and film, eventually leading to the amazing opportunities he's attracting to this day. He's now living his life doing exactly what he dreamed of years ago, the exact thing his rational conscious mind had convinced him, for so long, wasn't possible.

Any time we have a desire, our conscious mind creates a path from point A (where we are now) to point B (our desire - where we want to be). We then take action on that path. Want to be an engineer at IBM? The conscious mind comes up with that path. Graduate from high school, get the right college degree, find references, a job opening, land an interview, impress the interviewers, accept the position.

But what happens if that path isn't working? What if you can't figure out a way to get from step 3 to step 4, and you can't come up with a solution or way around it? You then believe that achieving your goal is not possible. You form the perspective that there's no way to get there, and that is when you feel stuck.

> **What most people don't realize (or forget) is that the conscious mind's path is irrelevant. It's meaningless.**

Calvin felt stuck because he believed that he had to spend two years in New York and do a $20,000 training to achieve his goal, which wasn't feasible for him. He felt stuck.

The truth is that Calvin, or anyone else, is never stuck. The path to your desire is irrelevant to the path created by the conscious mind, because achieving the desire is about vibration. As long as you can match the vibration of the desire, it must appear. It must manifest. This applies to jobs, money, relationships. Anything in physical reality.

By this understanding, since you are the only one who controls your vibration, you never are and can never be stuck.

(By the way, if you've been feeling that stuck feeling, this is your permission to once and for all let it go.)

I'm going to repeat that once again, for clarity's sake.

That feeling of being stuck is due to a false perception that you can't get from here to there because you're forgetting that getting there is about nothing other than vibration, and you have the full power to shift your vibration and match that place you really want to be.

> **You aren't stuck. You never have been, and never will be, stuck. You're simply re-creating the stuck experience, and you can let that go.**

The third key point around money, is a simple yet common trap most people who struggle with finances and debt fall under. Most people are trying to work their way out of debt and lack, rather than into wealth.

Any time you're pushing against anything, you're giving momentum to it. Any time you put focus on anything you don't want, you're drawing more of it into your physical reality.

When it comes to money (like anything else), there's two sides of a coin. The presence of money, and the absence of it. Every single time you think the thought, "I don't have enough for this," "I don't have enough for that," "that's too expensive," "the money's not there," and other similar statements, you're practicing the lack side of the coin, propagating that cycle.

Even a subtle statement such as "I'll buy that thing when the money shows up" is practicing the vibration of "right now I don't have the money," which once again, adds momentum to the experience of not having the money.

Instead, you want to work yourself into the vibration of wealth and abundance. How do you do that when the money's not there? Simple – practice wealth and money on topics other than money. Spend time noticing and appreciating the wealth of amazing friends.

The abundance of clean water and oxygen.

The abundance of love expressed by your kids.

The wealth of knowledge accessible at your fingertips.

The abundance of tomatoes in your garden.

Practicing these vibrations will carry over beyond these topics, into your finances. Be cautious, however – you need to stay off the topic of lack in parallel. Every time you notice wealth and abundance, you take a step towards more wealth and financial abundance. Every time you notice absence or lack, you take a step away from wealth and financial abundance.

This is one simple example of something you can start practicing to help appreciate your financial circumstance. In the next chapter, we're going to get more practical and I'll share with you my best tips for manifesting more money.

CHAPTER KEY CONCEPT SUMMARY

- Money is not the enabler of experiences – your vibration is.

- Money can not prevent you from moving down your path of least resistance. If money needs to manifest for your next step, as long as you are a vibrational match, it will show up.

- Most people are so concerned about making money show up, they aren't building momentum toward the thing they would use the money for.

- Give money a reason to manifest.

- The vibration of money is freedom.

15

HOW TO ALLOW MORE MONEY IN THE BANK

On the last Abraham Hicks Caribbean cruise, we spent a week on the Celebrity Edge, one of the newest and most advanced cruise ships on the ocean. While onboard, we spent some time browsing in some of the watch shops, where we tried on gorgeous watches in the $40,000 price range.

At that time, I wasn't quite ready to spend that amount of money on a watch, but my intent was to soon own a piece that I could wear as a reminder of my high level of vibrational wealth (which we all have) to boost that momentum. Fast forward to this past week, I was gifted a watch for my birthday by my beautiful 10-year-old daughter.

It was her idea to get me a watch. She picked it out all by herself, and it's the perfect piece which I could have never found on my own.

It's not a popular or designer brand. The time is slightly off and needs to be adjusted most mornings. It makes a nice loud ticking sound. It may not have diamonds, gold plating, a high price tag, or some kind of Swiss certificate of authenticity, but it's an even better reminder of the wealth I have in my own life. This watch is worth 1000x more than the Cartier, Panerai and Hublot watches I've seen or tried on aboard ship.

WEALTH ISN'T JUST ABOUT MONEY

A strongly practiced vibration on one topic will spread to others. When you tune into the vibration in one aspect of your life, that frequency of wealth will directly infuse that feeling and vibration of wealth into other aspects such as money, friendships, or free time.

One of my favorite tips for creating positive momentum and boosting finances is to practice the vibration of wealth. Not necessarily in the financial department, but spending time noticing the wealth of love you receive from your kids, your parents or a partner. The wealth of beautiful people or friendships in your life. The wealth of good water to drink, or time to do what you want. Practicing those vibrations of wealth, and holding steady in them, will directly impact the wealth in all aspects of life, including finances.

Want more money? Here's my guide to making it happen. In this chapter you'll find more of my top tips and key aspects for anyone looking to shift their financial circumstance in a positive way.

First and foremost, alignment. I know you're likely getting sick and tired of me telling you to get into alignment. But here it is again, yet another reminder – your first priority, before working your way into anything, should be alignment.

PRACTICE THE VIBRATION OF FREEDOM

You can't attract circumstances that bring relief from the vibration of struggle.

You can't attract lasting success from the energy of failure.

You can't attract satisfying experiences from dissatisfaction.

So what about money? What vibrational frequencies match the experiences of financial wealth and abundance? Freedom and abundance.

Ask almost anyone suffering from a lack of financial prosperity how their circumstance makes them feel, and the most likely answer is, stuck.

"I can't do what I want, I feel stuck."

"I can't figure it out, I don't know what to do, I feel stuck."

"There's no way out, the debt just keeps getting worse, I'm stuck."

When you ask the probing question, "How do my financial circumstances make me feel?" what answer comes up for you? If stuck is your answer, on a zero to ten scale, how intense is that stuck feeling? The stronger that emotion, the more important the clearing work and working your way to the opposite end of the stick – that feeling of freedom.

If a different answer other than stuck showed up for you, that may not be wrong either. As mentioned before, everyone is a unique fingerprint of experiences resulting in different perspectives and layers of emotions. Regardless of what emotion surfaced, if it has a high level of intensity, maybe a five or greater, you'll want to do some clearing work or processes to help move into a better-feeling place. You can do this using the clearing processes outlined in this book or seek out help from a well- trained practitioner.

WORK YOUR WAY INTO WEALTH, NOT OUT OF LACK

Most people looking for a positive financial shift are trying to work their way out of lack, out of not having enough money. By now, hopefully you understand that you can't work your way out of anything, only into something. The minute you try to work your way out, you're pushing against it, and giving momentum to that very thing you're trying to get away from.

> **Any time you have the thoughts "How am I going to pay this?" "I don't have enough money for that," "How do I pay off that loan?" or "I owe this," you're giving more momentum and propagating these experiences.**

What you want to do is counter these by shifting these statements into ones about where you want to be.

For example, when you have the thought," How do I repay that $20,000 loan?" where is it that you really want to be? You want to be debt free. But even the thought of being debt free implies a vibration of debt. Instead, identify what your life would look like from the flip side of that coin.

What amount of money would you need to drop into your bank account, today, to bring you to a place of ease and relief? $20,000? $50,000? $100,000?

What would your life look like? How would you feel? What actions would you take? This is the other financial side of the spectrum from where you now stand. Reach for that. Bookmark that vision, that place. Embody it. Give it a label if you need to. Call it My Life 2.0. Make the money game about reaching for this place and the relief it brings — set your sights on being there.

Another way to achieve the vibrational frequency of wealth, the feeling of being wealthy, is to practice it. Similar to the abundance exercise in the previous chapter, how much wealth can you recognize in your reality?

EXPLORE SPLIT ENERGY (MONEY FEARS)

Second to emotions and perspectives, it is also important to explore fears which create split energy and self-sabotage around money manifestation.

Take Jenna, for example.

Jenna came to me because she recognized a self-sabotaging behaviour with regard to the success of her business. Jenna was a brilliant entrepreneur who would always find ways to mess things up, just as she was poised on the verge of major success. As a general rule, she rarely made mistakes and only seemed to make them, big ones, when significant financial gains were a potential result.

After a little digging, Jenna shared with me that at the tender age of ten, she lost her father to a sudden illness. Even though she implied she had done significant emotional work around the passing of her father, this flagged my suspicion. She explained that he was a businessman and the family was very wealthy. Her dad had invested the entire family fortune on what he anticipated to be a sure-shot deal. Unfortunately, he was wrong. The deal failed and the family lost its entire fortune. Jenna's father, heartbroken from the incident, developed post-traumatic stress and suddenly passed away as the result of a heart attack.

The trauma from this event caused Jenna's subconscious mind, wanting to keep her safe, to flag money as a threat to safety. It blamed wealth for the death of her father. At this moment, outside of Jenna's awareness, a self-sabotaging fear was now born, impacting her business and her ability to achieve financial success.

Another practical example of how fears can impact your finances comes from Linda, a businesswoman who came to me because her five-figure monthly income had dwindled to almost nothing over the course of a year. She wanted to understand the deeper cause and what was responsible for her financial problem. The answer very quickly became apparent. She was unhappy with the way her husband was spending money. Her husband was an intimidating man who had unhealthy spending habits of which Linda didn't approve. His large stature intimidated her, and she had fears of speaking up about the spending problem, so her subconscious mind found its own solution – spend the money before her husband has a chance to get his hands on it.

These simple examples of subconscious self-sabotage aren't the only ways we block finances. Split energy, as we looked at in the context of relationships, is just as important to explore around money. During my live seminars, we often do probing work around financial blocks. It's not uncommon to uncover well over a dozen common fears shared by audience members.

I'll screw it up. People will try and take advantage of me. I'll lose it all. I'll become a target. My family will get bitter and jealous. I'll be judged. I'll need to be different. My values might change. People who are wealthy are selfish. I'll have to be responsible for family or other people. Etc.

These are all common fears responsible for split energy that can create an energetic barrier, resistance, preventing you from allowing money in. Use the following probing statement to uncover your sources of split energy:

"If I had a large amount of money show up tomorrow, how would it feel unsafe?" "If I had a large amount of money show up tomorrow, what's the worst thing that could happen?"

Any responses that immediately come to mind are potential sources of split energy. Use the clearing processes in this book or work with a trained practitioner to clear them.

MIND THE VIBRATIONAL GAP

Everyone wants to win the lottery. Why try to manifest $5,000, when you can reach for $500,000,000, right?

Manifesting a large sum of money is no different than a small sum, unless you perceive it differently, which most people do.

> **The bigger the amount of money you're looking to manifest, the greater the chance of disbelief in the possibility of that manifestation happening.**

In the next twenty-four hours, how highly do you believe you can manifest $5? What about $50? $500? $5,000,000?

The greater the number, the bigger the doubt. The greater the doubt, the more resistance stands between you and manifestation creating a bigger gap that you need to jump, in order to allow that money to show up.

My advice when it comes to choosing a number is not to go too small, nor too big. Choose a number that brings a certain level of excitement and relief and start there. As that number begins to manifest, your confidence will grow, and with it, you can begin to grow your expectation of what will show up next.

RELEASE THE HOW

Often times I work with coaches who are struggling to manifest clients. When I ask them what their monthly goal might be, they'll say they want to manifest five clients and make $15,000 a month.

But here's the thing.

By attaching the client goal to the money goal, you're taking resistance from one topic and applying it to both.

If the intent you set is to manifest $15,000 per month through client work, if you have resistance to manifesting new clients (a fear of putting yourself out there, perhaps) then the client block is also a money block.

If you have split energy preventing you from manifesting money, you'll also experience the inability to attract clients (or if you do, you'll likely end up with a long list of unpaid invoices).

My advice in this context is to split money intent from career, business, and other topics. Set your intent for how much money you want to manifest, and that it manifests in easy and effortless ways that align with you. Parallel to that, set your intent for manifesting clients and client relationships that are fun, easy, fulfilling, and bring satisfaction to everyone involved.

CHAPTER KEY CONCEPT SUMMARY

- Alignment should be your number one priority on the quest for manifesting more money.

- Practice the vibrations of freedom and abundance.

- Work into wealth, not out of lack.

- Work through your money fears which create split energy.

- Don't reach too big, or you'll be creating a big vibrational gap which may be hard to jump.

- Let go of the how.

- Don't attach money to other goals. If you work as a coach, make money manifestation intent separate from client manifestation intent.

16

A GUIDE TO MANIFESTING HEALTH

Disclaimer: I am in no way a medical professional making medical claims. My background is in computer science, I teach about the Laws of the Universe, I write books, I speak, and I make people cry for a living (in a good way – by helping them release emotions). I am not a doctor, nor am I even close to being one (I didn't even take high school biology).

However.

Over the last five or six years, I have had numerous clients work with me with the intent of shifting physical ailments. In this chapter, I share my experiences and a small handful of the physical shifts I have witnessed through mental and emotional work founded in law of attraction principles. I will also share my viewpoints on the law of attraction, vibration, and its impacts on the physical body.

Overcoming health concerns and issues is the third of the three major elements that draw people to studying the law of attraction. Why? Because your physical body is also representative of your vibration.

Take Melanie for example.

Living in the UK, Melanie is a prominent businesswoman in her mid-forties who found me through one of my books. She had only just begun learning about the law of attraction and felt the immediate need to reach out. For three years, Melanie had been suffering from intense pain, which was diagnosed as an autoimmune disease. When I asked Melanie to describe the severity of her pain on a 0 to 10 scale (0 being low and 10 being high), she said it would fluctuate between 7 and 9, and could barely remember what it felt like to be pain-free. She also had been on a high dosage of pain medication for nearly two years.

Within six weeks of her first session with me, she had her first pain-free day. Twelve weeks later, aside from an occasional bad day, she was off medication and the pain was virtually gone. How did Melanie experience such a drastic shift in her physical state in such a short period of time?

First, we addressed the fears. Fears around healing and being healthy, and fears around letting the condition go. On occasion, I run into clients who have formed beliefs that they're better off keeping a condition, that in some way it keeps them safe from an unwanted circumstance. This is known as secondary gain and must first be addressed before underlying root causes can be released.

Second, we addressed beliefs around its not being possible to heal, and 'this won't work for me.'

Third, we identified the mental-emotional root causes, the underlying perspectives responsible for tuning into the vibrational frequency that matched the experience she had manifested. I did this using the pattern technique to identify dominant negative emotions I've shared earlier in this book. I also asked Melanie what had been going on in her life just prior to when the circumstance had begun. Roughly five to six weeks prior to when the pain started, she had experienced a severe emotional trauma. These clues led me to identify what emotions and underlying perspectives we needed to work on in order to release the condition.

Our next step, of course, was the clearing work which consisted of a mashup of the perspective-shifting technique from this book (working through the layers process) and Emotional Freedom Technique (EFT/Tapping). This step was the bulk of the work helping to shift her vibrational frequency back to a natural state of health.

The last step, which was done in parallel to the clearing work, was a four to five minute guided hypnosis I instructed her to use as often as possible, even hourly for the first week. This may seem excessive, but it was necessary. Here's why.

The pain in her body seemed to have been created by the cells having taken on a fight-or-flight state. Instead of naturally being relaxed, her body had made being tense and rigid the new default, which is enforced at a subconscious level. When the trauma had first occurred three years prior, she was in the fight-or-flight state for so long, she practiced being tense so much, it became her default.

After we dealt with the root causes, we needed to reprogram her body back to a relaxed state. This was done by getting her to repetitively tell her body to relax, through a short but powerful guided audio.

Melanie's story is not uncommon. I've seen multiple similar shifts with various types of conditions. I often wonder how different the medical system would look if people truly understood the impact of our mental-emotional state on the physical body.

Here is a short list of varying conditions and resulting shifts I've witnessed in some of the clients I've worked with.

AUTO-IMMUNE DISEASE

As seen in Melanie's story, my experience when it comes to these types of conditions seems to relate to the body's being in a tense state. In my experience, the root cause relates to strong emotions of not being good enough, the need to be perfect, the fears that it's not safe to make a mistake or to screw up. These conditions, especially Fibromyalgia, seem to be extremely responsive to positive shifts when dealing with emotional root causes.

IRRITABLE BOWEL SYNDROME (IBS)

Almost every client that I've worked with who suffers from IBS had what I call "walking on eggshell syndrome." An anticipation fear, where you're always worried about something or waiting for the other shoe to drop. This is often rooted in a childhood in which you grew up with someone who may have been unpredictable or even abusive and who could be triggered at any time, making you feel unsafe. It could also have come from an unhealthy relationship or having been bullied in school. Even when we grow out of the situation or step away from it, we carry the fear conditioning with us. Dealing with the root causes and working the client out of the anticipation fears typically results in a positive shift in the condition.

HEADACHES AND MIGRAINES

Those who suffer from headaches and migraines often have poor personal boundaries and feel unsafe speaking up or hold back, feeling obliged to compromise themselves, what they want, and do things they may not want to do.

INFERTILITY

I once worked with a client who went through years of failed IVF treatments and was told by doctors there was less than 1% chance she could conceive naturally. We spent a number of sessions that involved clearing fears around birth and labor from past trauma, clearing emotions around grief and sadness, and beliefs around it not being possible. A short time later I found out she conceived, naturally, and now has a beautiful baby boy.

DEPRESSION AND ANXIETY

Although not physical conditions, I've had a very high success rate in assisting men and women with these diagnosed conditions. I even witnessed one gentleman release a lifelong condition diagnosed as general anxiety in less than an hour. When it comes to depression, it's typically a momentum game that involves dealing with the emotional root causes, the reasons someone may not want to release the sadness, while in parallel retraining the habitual thought patterns to ones more representative of positive emotional states. When it comes to anxiety, it's about working through the underlying perspectives holding the fears in place.

In a more general sense, you don't need a diagnosed condition to use your physical body as a breadcrumb to what may be in your attraction point. Here's a short list of common body parts and what they seem to indicate that you might have going on in your vibration.

NECK AND SHOULDERS

Underlying emotions of feeling under pressure, not good enough, stress and possible perfectionism tendencies or feeling like it isn't safe to make a mistake.

LOWER BACK

Underlying emotions around fears of losing control, feeling stuck and powerless.

KNEES AND ELBOWS

Fears or indecision around direction, moving forward and other people's opinions or judgements about a path or direction you may be considering. Uncertainty around career, relationship or other aspects in your life. These conditions also seem to relate to dominant negative emotions of anger.

SKIN CONDITIONS

Skin conditions typically relate to feeling anger, frustration or irritation.

WEIGHT

Do you eat well and exercise but still struggle to lose weight? The third key piece to weight loss that very few people know about, is the importance of deep sleep. When you enter the deepest level of sleep, your body goes into what is known as rest and repair mode. If you don't enter rest and repair mode it becomes very difficult for your body to lose fat. Waking up tired, even after a long night sleep, is an indication that you aren't getting into a deep sleep at night. This is caused by stress and adrenal fatigue. When assisting clients with anxiety and clearing fears such as anticipation fear, it's not uncommon for them to suddenly start losing weight.

MANIFESTING BETTER HEALTH - TAKE ACTION

If you're looking to achieve better health by addressing the issue from a vibrational standpoint, these are the action steps or key points you can consider. Remember, however, these are not a replacement for modern healthcare. If you suffer from depression for example, there is no harm in seeking out professional help and medication that will help you feel better. From a place of feeling better, you're then better-suited to effectively deal with the root causes.

1. Reach for where you want to be, focusing on the feeling of health and relief rather than being focused on the energy of the problem.

2. Identify and shift the emotional root cause (mainly fears and dominant negative emotions).

3. Seek rest and relaxation to help your body to shift into rest and repair mode. Deal with any stress and pressure preventing you from a good night sleep, which you need to get your body into rest and repair mode.

4. Prepare and embody the healthy you.

5. Get the help you need. Don't be afraid to resort to various types of practitioners, regardless of what judgements others may have. Deep down only you know what feels best for you.

CONTRAST

17

I'VE DONE THE WORK, WHERE'S MY STUFF?

Contrast. The unwanted circumstances we face in our lives. How important of a topic is contrast in the context of the law of attraction? Understanding contrast is no less important than the other key topics we've explored so far in this book such as alignment, vibration, allowing, action, and acceleration.

Life will never be free of contrast. Without contrast, the ever-expansive nature of your own personal growth and movement towards your desire would cease to a halt. Contrast is what pushes you to ask for more. Contrast is the spark that triggers new awareness. Contrast, albeit uncomfortable and typically unwelcomed, is an essential part of the unfolding and core ingredient of the physical reality experience. I would go as far as saying that without it, the process of physical reality would have no point.

In this chapter, I'm going to teach you what contrast is really about and hopefully by the end of the next few pages you'll have a new appreciation for it and welcome it with open arms. We're then going to explore how to handle the painful contrast you experience when desires you seek aren't showing up.

UNDERSTANDING THE PURPOSE OF CONTRAST

When an unwanted circumstance occurs, maybe the unexpected ending of a relationship or the painful absence of a desire, the old paradigm mindset is the belief that you have, or are, screwing up. You've done something wrong. You've manifested a circumstance you do not want, something that is not preferred. You then feel stuck, you may be hard on yourself and engage in negative self-talk. There is also often an underlying belief that now you need to start over.

A Power Manifestor living in the new paradigm, however, understands that this couldn't be any further from the truth.

Here's why.

There is no such thing as backward movement. You can only ever move forward. Contrast is no indication of failure, it's simply an indication that the process to the desire you really want, is still in progress. The contrast you are experiencing is part of that process. It's a necessary ingredient in the unfolding towards the end desire you truly want. What you are perceiving as failure is not failure, it is a necessary step in the unfolding to the desire.

> **The true purpose of contrast is refinement.**
> **Refinement of your vibration.**
> **Refinement around the clarity of your desire.**

Again, contrast is not a failure. Contrast is a necessary steppingstone needed as part of the process to aid you in refining your vibration and the clarity to match what you truly want.

Take relationships for example.

Let's say you have your first boyfriend or girlfriend at the age of fourteen. In the two months of your first relationship with your first partner, you're going to realize what you did and didn't like in that relationship. You'll get clearer on what you want in both a partner and what you want out of a relationship.

A year or two later, you manifest your second partner. This person is a better fit than the last and doesn't have some of the unwanted qualities you noticed in your last relationship. This relationship may last five or six months. When it ends, you now have an even better idea of who or what you want in your next relationship.

With each relationship, you learn and grow. You become more aware of the type of person you eventually want to marry and have children with. How did the contrast of each failed relationship serve you?

They aided in the evolution of who you are and understanding what you truly want. Necessary steps of refinement towards the relationship that will ultimately match the relationship you desire.

Each relationship also triggered the refinement of your vibration. You may have had realizations and new awareness on topics such as self-worth, feeling good enough or deserving of a loving relationship. You may have learned about boundaries or the importance of self-love. This form of expansion is shifting you to a new vibrational place which would be a greater match to the relationship you really want.

Eventually, with the right inner work along the process of relationship after relationship, you continue to fine tune until you manifest your forever after.

When living in the new paradigm you don't only see that the unwanted is a necessary unfolding to achieving the wanted. You begin to appreciate and experience gratitude for contrast, from the understanding that contrast is the reason you find yourself having or moving towards the most cherished things in your life.

A power manifestor in the new paradigm understands that contrast is not the lack of forward movement. It's not the indication you've hit a brick wall. Forward movement is always happening at a vibrational level and the perceived lack of forward movement created by contrast in physical reality is only an illusion.

This may seem like a subtle shift in awareness, but the impact of this awareness is astronomical. When you perceive contrast as a negative thing, a brick wall, a step in the wrong direction, you're tuning into the vibration of lack of progress. This adds momentum to the physical reality experience of lack of progress. When you see the contrast as the forward movement it truly is, you then add momentum to the physical reality experience of forward movement.

WHEN A DESIRE ISN'T SHOWING UP

What happens when a desire isn't showing up? How do you deal with the unwanted circumstance of a desire not showing up when you've been chasing it for months, years or even a decade?

The first thing I remind clients who come to me looking for help after chasing a desire for a very long time is that their goal should be to embrace the new paradigm rather than chase desires. The second, is that there is no factor standing in the way of manifestation, other than what they have going on inside themselves.

Nothing can stand in the way of a desire, other than you.

There are no evil spirits or curses.
No past life implications.
No divine timing slowing things down (although there is an unfolding, no timing is set in stone).
Law of attraction is law. You must experience what you become a vibrational match to and there is no limitation to the tuning of your vibration.
The following triangle is what I call the Desire Realization Diagram. These are the three key areas of focus I explore with anyone who struggles with bringing in a specific desire. If being a Power Manifestor had a generalized formula, this would be it.

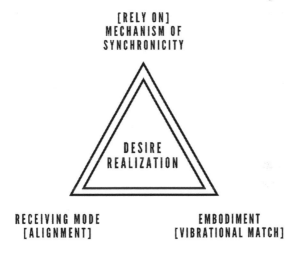

**[RELY ON]
MECHANISM OF
SYNCHRONICITY**

**DESIRE
REALIZATION**

**RECEIVING MODE
[ALIGNMENT]**

**EMBODIMENT
[VIBRATIONAL MATCH]**

1. The Mechanism of synchronicity.

A Power Manifestor understands that the unfolding of a desire from where you are to the realization of that desire is none of your business. The manifestation of a desire comes from you becoming a vibrational match to that desire and following inspired action and impulses. Everything else in between is handled by the mechanism of synchronicity. If you do not allow yourself to rely on that mechanism, you put yourself in the vibration of effort, in the energy of the problem and you're essentially putting the mechanism on the bench.

Your role is to literally chill out, feel good, enjoy life, follow inspired impulses when they show up and let the mechanism of synchronicity line up the rest.

> **The real difference between an amateur and a professional manifestor, is the ability to rely on and utilize this mechanism of synchronicity.**

2. Embodiment [Vibrational Match]

For a desire to realize, you need to become a vibrational match to it, there's no way around this.

Through the embodiment processes, by embodying the mental and emotional state as if the desire already exists, you tune to the frequency of it allowing the desire to show up. This is where the exploration of your attraction point, clearing emotions, working through split energy and shifting perspectives is important. This step is the bulk of the work for most people.

3. The Receiving Mode [Alignment]

Being in alignment is what puts you in the receiving mode for the inspired impulses and actions being fed to you from your inner being. The only benchmarks for your level of alignment and receiving mode are how good you feel and your level of satisfaction. Being in the receiving mode is the opposite of effort, struggle and trying to work yourself into your desires.

If you struggle with the manifestation of a specific desire, I suggest exploring each of these three points. Identify which of the three seems to be the most challenging for you and explore it in greater detail.

I've shared the desire realization diagram with my students in The Power Manifesting Collective. Many of them have printed the diagram as a reminder in their office or bedside. Some even joked of getting it tattooed on their arm. I see it as a daily reminder to remain focused on the vibrational nature of reality.

WHAT TO DO IF YOU STILL FEEL STUCK

Still feeling stuck? Here are some more probing questions you can ask that may help you further identify what could be getting in your way.

1. Are you in a state of desire, want or need? Are you chasing or allowing?

If you are too focused or obsessed with making something show up, you are likely blocking it through the focus of its absence. Are you in a state of want and need, energies of desperation akin to resistance, or are you in desire and excitement around the process and the unfolding?

If the thought of the desire brings excitement and enthusiasm, you are likely creating positive momentum. If the absence of the desire fuels negative emotions, you're likely creating negative momentum. In this case, work on staying off the topic as much as possible.

Desperation is an indication that your mind is attaching that specific outcome or desire to an emotional state it wants to achieve. How would you feel if you had that desire? How do you feel without it? What emotional void are you looking to soothe through this manifestation? Use these questions to identify the negative emotions you want to work out of as well as the positive emotions you want to work into.

2. Are you working your way out of or into?

Remember, by pushing against the unwanted, you're adding momentum to it. Are you pushing against the absence of a desire or an unwanted circumstance or are you clear on the outcome you desire and have you put your focus there?

3. Have you gotten clear and detailed on what you want the desire to look like?

Accelerate forward-moving momentum by getting clear on what you want or where you want to be. Jump to a point in the future where that desire has manifested and write about it in the fullest detail possible. Write in the present tense using as much emotion and all five senses.

Spend time embodying these desires using my guided embodiment meditation, speaking about them out loud as if they exist, writing about them or any other process that feels good for you.

4. Are you trying to make the money show up or are you building momentum towards the desire?

Money is one of the biggest manifestation killers. Not because it's hard to manifest, but because it prevents you from building momentum towards your desire because you're focused on the wrong thing. If you become a vibrational match to your desire, the desire needs to manifest no matter what you have in your bank account. The reverse is also true. No matter how much money you have, if you're not a vibrational match to something, it cannot manifest.

> **In a nutshell, put all your focus on building momentum toward the desire rather than what you believe you need to accomplish to make it show up.**

5. Are you more concerned about the desire than you are about feeling good?

If the answer is yes, then you've made yourself dependent on the desire to feel good and it's likely pulling you out of alignment. Get clear on what you want, do your intention setting and embodiment work, and then hand the desire over to an avatar to help let it go. There is nothing more that needs to be done other than focus on alignment, feeling good and working your way into the new paradigm.

6. Do you have any split energy?

If you had this desire, how does it feel unsafe? What's the worse thing that could happen? If specific fears come to mind, they may be creating split energy, which you'll want to work through.

7. Are you a vibrational match?

In what way are you not a vibrational match to the desire? How does the absence make you feel? How does the stuck situation in which you find yourself make you feel? Work your way out of these emotions into their positive setpoints (i.e. from stuck to free, not good enough to good enough, etc.).

CHAPTER KEY CONCEPT SUMMARY

- Life will never be free of contrast, it's part of the ever-evolving nature of physical reality and your own expansion.

- Contrast is a necessary part of the unfolding and should be seen as a refinement step during the manifestation process.

- The serving purpose of contrast is the refinement in the clarity of your desires as well as the refinement of your vibration.

- Contrast is not the indication of failure of backwards movement. This perspective slows down momentum towards your desire.

- Forward movement is always happening at a vibrational level and a Power Manifestor is in appreciation of contrast as it helps with the refinement process and forward movement.

- When a desire isn't realizing, the three elements to explore at a higher level are the utilization of the mechanism of synchronicity, embodiment (vibrational match) and being in the receiving mode (alignment).

- The difference between an amateur manifestor and a professional is your ability to rely on the mechanism of synchronicity.

18

FROM SHIT TO SHIFT –
A STEP BY STEP GUIDE
TO DEALING WITH CONTRAST

I n the previous chapter, we explored the purpose of contrast and what to look at when a specific desire isn't
showing up. In this chapter, we are now going to look
at what specific action steps to take when you find yourself
experiencing contrast.

SEEK RELIEF

Our first step, as always, is to work your way out of the energy of the problem and back into alignment. If a particular
circumstance creating contrast is a dominant factor in your
life, there's a good chance you're largely practicing the vibration of struggle. What vibration should we reach for in the
face of struggle? Relief.

In our day-to-day life, any human on the planet would
agree they feel a wide range of emotions from the moment
they wake up to the moment they fall asleep. Angry. Sad.
Hopeless. Satisfied. Happy. Accomplished. The full list of

possible feelings would likely add a significant number to the page count of this book.

In order to simplify all these emotional states, I've categorized emotions into five distinct states of being which I've inserted into the following scale. It moves from the lowest vibration of struggle to the highest vibration of bliss.

BLISS

TURNED ON

SATISFACTION

RELIEF

STRUGGLE

What is the purpose of this scale and how do you use it?

Making small leaps in the way you feel is much easier than making large jumps. For example, someone who is in a state of struggle will have a much easier time reaching for relief than for bliss. This scale is a roadmap or guideline you can use to gradually work your way up to a better feeling place. Alignment begins as soon as you've found yourself dominantly in a state of relief and the more you work your way up that scale, the greater the momentum you create.

First, recognize your baseline. In which of these states do you spend most of your day-to-day life? Are you dominantly in struggle? Relief? Once you've identified your baseline, the next step is to practice reaching for and maintaining the next level above it.

If you're dominantly in Struggle, spend as much of your day as possible reaching for Relief.

If you're dominantly in Relief, reach for Satisfaction.

If you're dominantly in Satisfaction, Reach for Turned On.

If you're dominantly in Turned On, Reach for Bliss.

After doing a good job of practicing a specific setpoint for a certain period of time, it'll become your new baseline and feel natural. You'll notice that you're automatically staying there. Congratulations, you've just leveled up! You can now work your way up the next step along that scale.

Seeking relief sometimes also means taking action you may not want to take.

In the face of struggle, a common question often goes something like this:

"I've quit my corporate job to be a full-time coach, I have no income yet, and I'm struggling to pay the rent each month. What should I do? Doing a bit of contract work doesn't feel good and I'm not passionate about it, but struggling with money doesn't feel good either."

Someone in this position isn't likely a vibrational match to attract clients and is stuck in a very wobbly position. What advice would you give?

My advice is to take whatever action, even if it isn't ideal, that will bring you relief. You want to minimize the wobble to work your way back up that scale into relief and satisfaction where you're in a better-feeling place of alignment and in your power. Even if going back to a corporate job doesn't feel like the most exciting and desirable action, if it brings you to relief from struggle, it's a step in the right direction.

GET OUT OF THE ENERGY OF THE PROBLEM

One of the tips I gave you around money was to work your way into wealth, not out of debt. Any time we're trying to work our way out of anything, we're adding momentum to that thing we're trying to move away from. This doesn't only apply to money, but all types of contrast.

Are you pushing against being single?

Are you pushing against not having enough money for rent at the end of the month?

Are you pushing against a medical condition you can't quite figure out how to solve?

Set a reminder if needed every morning, or a few times a day, to point and keep your focus on where you want to be, rather than toward what you don't want. Remember, the new paradigm is about approaching the problem from a vibrational standpoint rather than an efforting standpoint of trying to do everything you can to fix or figure it out, activating a current reality loop.

Keep in mind, however, that I'm not telling you to keep a blind eye to the problem. Sometimes you'll recognize that a certain piece of action may be necessary to curb you back towards relief. There is still balance to practice between completely ignoring a problem, giving constant attention to the problem, and putting your focus and building momentum to what you truly want.

A final reminder on the topic of pushing against is to remember that no matter how bad the contrast feels, there is a purpose behind it and it is there, in some way, to serve you. It can be a launching point for growth and expansion, and the more you can practice being okay with the contrast, the more you can appreciate it as a process that is designed to help uplevel you, the quicker you will move through it.

GET CLEAR ON WHAT YOU WANT

You can't set your sails towards where you want to be if you haven't decided and gotten clear on a destination. If you haven't gotten clear on what you do want, it's going to be much harder to focus away from the problem.

Jump a few weeks or months into the future to a point where you've manifested where you want to be. Write about it in the present tense. The feelings you feel, what you see, using all five senses describing the scene in as much detail as possible.

Your next step is to embody that vibration as much as you can throughout the day. You can also use my embodiment meditation provided in the bonus companion content to assist you with this process.

ACKNOWLEDGE YOU CREATED IT

You are not a victim to anything other than the vibration you're putting out. Remember that by taking ownership for having created this contrast, you are empowering yourself to change it. Acknowledge that you've been creating a circumstance that you do not prefer, and just as you created it by practicing one vibration, you can uncreate it by practicing another. Owning will help put you in your power.

EXPLORE YOUR ATTRACTION POINT

When a contrasting circumstance seems to be ongoing much longer than it should, it's always because of one of two reasons.

1. You're stuck in a current reality loop.

2. You are tuned into a vibration you keep practicing.

We discussed the current reality loop in a past chapter. You simply keep creating more of what you focus on, and the act of focus on a current reality circumstance that is unwanted will keep creating more of it. This is the reason behind the importance of getting clear on where you want to be and putting your focus there.

If you're practicing an unwanted vibration, you'll want to spend some time identifying what that vibration might be so you can work your way out of it. In order to do this, I suggest using the pattern technique from earlier in this book where you look at different circumstances in your reality and identify the negative emotions they each bring up. This exercise will help you identify your dominant negative emotions, which most likely match the vibration of the circumstance you are experiencing. If this is the case, you engage in the perspective-shifting process to work your way out of the vibration.

WHEN ALL ELSE FAILS, TAKE A NAP

When all is said and done, the ultimate benchmark for anything law of attraction is how you feel. When you feel weighed down by the heaviness of contrast, work your way towards the best feeling thing you can do in order to feel better. Take a nap. Visit a friend. Go to the beach or hit the gym. Contrast is a normal part of the human experience, it's part of what you came here for. Without it, there would be no growth, no expansion, nothing to reach for. It's not a sign you screwed up or that you've done anything wrong. It's simply part of the process of your own evolution and as a leading edge creator of your own reality you have the full ability to move through and to the other side of it.

CHAPTER KEY CONCEPT SUMMARY

- The first step when hit by contrast or if you find yourself dominantly in the energy of struggle, is to seek relief.

- Are you in the energy of the problem? Are you constantly pushing against what you don't want or are you focused on where you want to be?

- Get clear on what you want so that you have a direction to point your sails in.

- Explore your attraction point – are you stuck in a current reality loop or is there a vibration you keep practicing?

- When all else fails, take a nap, go watch a movie, find something to do to break the momentum and get off the topic.

19

WHEN PEOPLE PULL YOU DOWN – HOW TO STOP OTHERS FROM LOWERING YOUR VIBE

"Nick, how do you stay aligned and focused on your wealth and abundance vibe if your partner has different beliefs and it keeps knocking you out of your energy? Do you just keep practicing daily until you build a strong wealthy vibe muscle?"

This is a question I recently received as a direct message on one of my social media accounts. When it comes to maintaining your alignment and feeling good, one of the biggest factors that seems to weigh people down is other people.

So, what do you do about it? You essentially have three options.

Option one: sell your home and live in seclusion in a cave in the middle of nowhere so nobody can find or trigger you.

Option two: try to change every single person you ever need to interact with so that their actions and behaviors accommodate your belief system in a way that is most appealing to you.

Option three: adjust your own beliefs and perspectives in ways that you no longer become triggered by other people.

You can't spend the rest of your life in a cave, nor can you spend the rest of your life trying to change everyone else. Of these options, the only sane and feasible choice, then, is option number three. Such an important choice, in fact, that I've dedicated an entire chapter to this topic.

If I were to categorize how we allow others to impact our vibration and or alignment, I could categorize how people pull us down into three distinct categories.

1. Other people's behavior

2. Poor boundaries

3. Feeling responsible for other people

WHEN OTHER PEOPLE PULL YOU DOWN

A number of years ago I had attended a conference in Atlanta where I had the privilege of hearing one of my favorite authors, Carolyn Myss, speak. Carolyn, in her late fifties or early sixties, came on stage with a very strong and stern energy. Before she even spoke a single word, you could tell she had something important to say, and she didn't look happy about it.

As she stepped up to the microphone, some of the very first words that came out of her mouth, were these:

"How dare you put the responsibility of your own happiness on somebody else's shoulders?"

She literally, and passionately, went on a twenty-minute rant in the same way an old school teacher would discipline a misbehaving classroom. Looking around the sold-out auditorium with over a thousand attendees, jaws were dropping left, center and right. The blissful and zen-like energy created earlier in the day from peaceful speakers such as Wayne Dyer, was no more. The love- and light-seeking audience was just brought back down to reality with a vibrational slap in the face.

Carolyn delivered the message in a stern, yet graceful and loving way. Most of the audience was taken aback by her message. Over the course of the two days with nearly a dozen different speakers consisting of many of the best-selling authors in self-help, this was the message that had the greatest impact. Why? Because she was right.

> **If you're like most people, the number one reason other people lower your vibration is because they aren't behaving the way you want them to behave. End of story.**

They frustrate you because they didn't clean the kitchen when you wanted it done. They pull you down because they don't believe in law of attraction and judge you for making alignment a priority rather than working hard. They're angry all the time about small things they shouldn't be angry about. They have different political perspectives than you do. They aren't buying you flowers, giving you words of affirmation or taking you out for dinner as often as you think they should.

In a nutshell, they aren't who you think they should be.

It might be a spouse, a partner, a family member or even a neighbor. It doesn't matter how they are connected to you. Nobody's behavior is your concern (unless it's harmful to you, which we'll soon address), and nobody else is responsible for your emotional state or happiness.

If Paul wants to be an angry person, he has the right to be an angry person. If Gina wants to be judgmental and criticizing towards people around her, that's her choice too.

If you think it is Sara's job to make you feel loved, worthy, or good enough; it's not.

You need to take ownership for how you feel, and stop blaming them, because they aren't the problem. Then what's the problem? The problem is never the circumstance (which in this case is other people). The problem is how you internally respond to the circumstance (those people).

> **People aren't lowering your vibration or pulling you from your alignment. It's your perspectives about them or the way they treat you that pull you down.**

It's not Paul's anger. It's your perspective about his anger and behavior being wrong or inappropriate. It's not Gina's criticizing. It's your own emotional wounds she triggers through her judgements. It's not Sara's lack of positive reinforcement, it's your own feelings of negative perceptions about yourself. I'm going to repeat this one more time. It's not them – it's you.

But that's a good thing, and here's why.

If they truly were the problem, you'd have to spend your entire life trying to change other people, every single person around you, to be who you want them to be in order to maintain a high state of alignment and prevent them from dragging you down. How easy would that be? If you're like most people you've likely already been doing that and may have come to the realization that it's impossible.

The only true solution is to work on you and your triggers when it comes to other people, which is something you can do. Learn to understand that they aren't the caretakers of your happiness. They aren't responsible for being who you want them to be. Their judgements of you are meaningless and based on their own emotional wounds. Even though you may not agree with their behavior or the decisions they make, they are doing the best they know how at their level of awareness. Everyone is, even if they are acting out of their fears or pain body. There may be a better path for them, and they may not see it, but you need to learn and accept who they are and their journey. The more you can do so, the more you'll detach and the less of an impact they will have over your alignment.

EXPRESS YOUR BOUNDARIES

What if someone else's behavior is impacting you in a negative way? What if they're voting for a new class president who wants to force the entire class to purchase five hundred dollars worth of textbooks each, which nobody really needs? What happens when the end result of someone else's behavior is going to force you into a circumstance that you don't want?

When you understand the vibrational nature of reality, you understand this isn't a concern.

Why? Because there isn't a single person on this planet who can touch your vibration, other than you, and you cannot experience a circumstance that is not a match to your vibration.

If you feel like you've ever been forced into a circumstance or experienced something that you do not want, it's because in some way, you had to be a vibrational match to it. You may not understand how or why, but to deny this would be to deny the existence of the law of attraction. Remember, gravity takes no exceptions. We don't see rare occurrences of people or objects suddenly floating off into space. The law of attraction doesn't make any exceptions either.

> ## It doesn't matter if it's the President of the United States, your brother, or your best friend. Nobody can force you into an unwanted circumstance — they can only be attracted through your own vibration.

Boundaries are also important when it comes to speaking up or standing up for yourself. Often it isn't just the behavior of other people that might pull you from your alignment, but their negative or harsh behavior towards you. It could be verbal. It could be physical. Although the circumstance may be something you've attracted through your vibration, it doesn't mean that if it doesn't feel good or sabotages your alignment, that you need to put up with it.

Unfortunately, many people do.

Why? Fear.

Fear of being rejected or attacked.

Fear of being alone or abandoned.

Fear of hurting the person who may be attacking you.

It could be one of these fears, or potentially many others. As previously mentioned, we've all grown up having a set of experiences with different fears and beliefs. If I were to list all the fears around boundaries I've seen in clients, it could double the size of this book.

If you recognize that you're a victim of someone else's behavior or struggle in speaking up or having a voice, try the following probing question.

> *If I do speak up or say what needs to be said, how does this feel unsafe, and what's the worst thing that could happen?*

Whatever fears come to mind, you'll want to work through the layers and use reframing as explained in the earlier chapters of this book.

Another consideration is that if you're attracting circumstances where people treat you a certain way, they are match to your vibration. If you carry emotions of unworthiness and not being good enough, you will likely attract people who reflect these emotions back to you. If you leave a relationship where your partner brought up those emotions, you'll want to work those out of your vibration so that you don't re-attract similar scenarios.

LIFTING OTHER PEOPLE UP

The third of the common alignment killers when it comes to other people, is when other people experience contrast, and have the false belief that we're responsible for lifting them up.

In a previous chapter, we discussed how you came here to live life for you. But somehow, we often take on the role or responsibility of the contrast that other people may be experiencing. We're not talking about necessities of life or your role of a parent making sure your kids are fed or make it to school on time. To be blunt, what we're talking about here is trying to solve other people's problems for them.

Why do we so desperately need, or find ourselves in a position where we take on that responsibility or put it on our own shoulders?

Because the discomfort of others triggers our own discomfort.

When a loved one struggles in any aspect of their life, whether it be depression, a struggle to land a job, or failing math, it's tough. As a parent, when my child hurts, it's not easy to watch. But we can't forget that just as our contrast is serving our own growth and expansion, so is theirs.

Earlier in this chapter I told you that if you're on the quest to change people to better suit who you want them to be so you can maintain your alignment, you're fighting a losing battle. This also applies to the circumstances other people are experiencing. You never can and never will be able to control the lives of other people, and that includes your children and your family. They didn't come here to make life decisions and have experiences within the bounds of what makes you feel safe and secure. They came here for their own set of experiences, which include not only positive growth and expansion, but contrast as well. By stepping into their flow and unfolding and interfering with their contrast, you're quite possibly sabotaging the purpose the contrast is meant to serve to them.

If I continue to tie my son's shoes for him, will he ever learn to tie his shoes? If I soothe my sister every time she finds herself ending a failed relationship, will she ever learn to soothe herself? If I take on the responsibility of uplifting my partner, compromising my needs to make her happy, will she ever learn to manage her own emotional state?

Helping others through their contrasting circumstance is, more often then not, as non-serving for them as it is for you.

Don't get me wrong, other people are part of the physical reality experience, and, yes, there are occasions when helping people is in your flow and serving for everyone involved. It's not about refusing to help people, but in checking in and asking yourself if you're acting out of efforted action or inspired action.

How do you know if it's out of effort? Helping that person feels like effort, it weighs you down, it's not in your flow, and you're doing it to uplift yourself or improve on the way you feel.

How do you know if it's out of inspiration? As explained in the chapter on action taking, you take the action for the enjoyment and inspiration to take the action, with no anticipation of what the outcome needs to look like. Under these circumstances it's often as if physical reality has created an organic rendezvous beneficial for those involved.

A final key point on uplifting and helping other people, an important concept I explain to my practitioners in training, is that either you can't or you don't have to.

Let me explain.

On any given topic, someone is either in the vibration of the problem or of the solution. If they are in the vibration of the problem, it doesn't matter what book they read, what coach they work with or what steps they take, they will not manifest the solution. If they are in the vibration of the solution, it doesn't matter what path they take – as long as they are in alignment, the solution will find them.

What does this mean in the context of feeling the need to help them or other people? You're off the hook. Why? Because if they're in the vibration of the problem, you can't help them. Because if they're in the vibration of the solution, even if you decide not to help them, they'll still attract the solution.

Even if you step in, and take action to solve a problem for someone, the contrast likely hasn't played out in a way that shifts the vibration of the person experiencing the contrast. They'll just re-attract it.

So, how do we best serve or uplift others who may be suffering in the face of contrast?

By living your best possible life. By maintaining your highest possible vibration, and by living your life for you. This will help to show others what's possible for their lives. You give them a permission slip to make themselves a priority, focus on feeling good for themselves, and live their best possible life.

You help others by serving you.

CHAPTER KEY CONCEPT SUMMARY

- When it comes to protecting your vibration from other people, your only choice is to adjust your own triggers so that others no longer impact you.

- It's not other people's responsibility to mold themselves or act in ways that are pleasing to you, nor is it your responsibility to uplift them.

- Nobody can force you into an unwanted circumstance – only your vibration can.

- Learn to exercise clear boundaries by dealing with the fears that prevent you from speaking up.

- It's not your responsibility to lift people up, and by doing so, you are likely compromising your own alignment.

20

LEAPING ONTO THE LEADING EDGE

D ifferent things excite different people. For me, nothing feels more exciting than pushing the boundaries of what's possible in physical reality. Exploring the nature of our individual potentials as humans. Exploring how we can bend reality in ways never seen before, exploring the depths of consciousness and who we truly are, and what the nature of physical reality truly is.

To break free from The Matrix, just as Neo did.

What does it mean, to me, to be on the leading edge?

It's fully embracing the new paradigm of living. It's breaking free from the mold of what we're taught about life and how to live it. It's about stepping away from how society believes we should be living our lives and embracing the guidance we receive from deep inside ourselves.

If you're like most people, you came to this book in search of manifestation, and there's nothing wrong with that. Desire is good – it's part of the experience.

But I suggest another path.

I suggest embracing life on the leading edge. Manifestation and desire are still part of the game, but their focus is no longer the primary intent. The new focus? Freedom. Joy. Ease. Synchronicity. Magic. Expansion. Abundance in all forms. Appreciation. Satisfaction. Alignment. Embrace releasing the struggle and effort for a new way of being where life evolves through a co-creative experience between you and your inner being.

In embracing the new paradigm and making it a priority, you'll be getting what you truly want. The manifestation will also show up with much more ease. The stuff is the conscious mind's belief as to how to achieve these with ease, flow, and freedom. Understand that you don't need those things to achieve that, that the mechanism of synchronicity and your inner being has it all taken care of. Your only job is to step back and relax into who you really are and make alignment your priority.

You may have noticed that much of what I've taught you so far in this book is about undoing. Removing the false beliefs and perceptions that hold us back.

Why? Because the journey of self-help and expansion is just that. It's a journey of re-discovering who we really are, our authenticity, honoring that authenticity, living it and in this process also discovering how powerful we really are as creators.

One of the biggest barriers we all face in this journey? Society.

When I reflect back on my forty years of existence in this physical body, there is no period of time that stands out more than ten months that spanned between 2011 and 2012.

The best way I can describe what comes to mind when I reflect back on this time, is that my entire life was thrown into a high-powered blender, cranked up to top speed, then spat back out.

During this time period I quit my six-figure corporate job. I left my marriage. I moved away to a small coastal town, a two-hour drive from my kids. I had had exactly what society tells you to strive for, on paper. A peaceful marriage. A dependable career. Two kids, a boy and a girl. Finances.

A beautiful home in a neighborhood which my brother had even labeled as Pleasantville, where I had fantastic neighbors and friends I frequently gathered with.

I followed my inner guidance, a pull I could not ignore, and left it all behind.

To this day, almost eight years later, most people from that time in my life still don't understand. Some verbally attacked me. Most haven't spoken to me since. They may never understand, and that's okay. I still cherish those friendships and miss them, even though I'm at a new place, living a new life that is more aligned with who I truly am.

Stepping away from what I call my old life and the old paradigm is without a doubt the hardest thing I've ever done. However, I believe that if I stayed, I would not have been honoring who I really am at the core of my being, and over time would have become complacent or maybe even sick.

Following your own flow, where your soul is calling you, and stepping out on the leading edge doesn't mean your path needs to look like mine. It doesn't mean you need to walk away from anything at all, and I'm not trying to scare you. Each and every one of our paths is different.

Why am I sharing this story?

I want to emphasize that the leading edge isn't called the leading edge because it's the same as what everyone else is doing or believing. It's called the leading edge because it's new. Because it's different than the norm. It's not how most people believe things should be.

And, if you want to truly live and stay on the leading edge, you need to be okay with that.

You need to accept that not everyone is going to be okay with the way you choose to live your life. Not everyone is going to see or understand the choices you make or why you make them. Not everyone understands the vibrational nature of reality and the new paradigm of living.

People might judge you.

People might criticize you.

A large pool of people will not understand you.

You never said, "I'm going to go into physical reality, in this physical body, to save someone else. To please other people. To make them the dominant priority over me."

You came here to live life for nobody else but you.

In any given moment, you have two choices.

Choice number one, play it safe. Keep other people pleased and do what other people want and expect of you. Keep them happy at your own expense. Oftentimes we do this out of fear of repercussion, of someone else's being displeased and taking it out on you.

Choice number two, honor who you are, your journey, and your flow. In this context, you need to be okay with other people being displeased. With other people not wanting you to do this or that, because it displeases them or they don't understand it.

How dare you date that person.

How dare you not go to college.

How dare you not come to the family gathering next week.

How dare you be so irresponsible.

How dare you go without me.

Pleasing other people is never your responsibility. In fact, people-pleasing in itself is a form of manipulation. When we people-please, we are manipulating a circumstance to please someone else. We are being manipulative, pleasing them over ourselves because their displeasure causes us discomfort.

If you want to fully step into the new paradigm and embrace life on the leading edge, you need to be okay with the discomfort of others. You need to be okay with them choosing to be displeased and not understanding. It's not your job to convince anyone of anything, and by trying to convince them to approve of your choices and your actions, you're only going to pull yourself down, and out of alignment.

After stepping into the new paradigm, many of my clients feel the need to help others. Their lives have had such a positive and drastic shift, they want to teach their parents, siblings, family and friends how to get into alignment and what's possible for them.

Most people, however, don't want to change. Growth, expansion and this type of awareness isn't on their path. They are okay with their struggles and what is. You need to be okay with that. Nobody likes to be told how to be or what to do, and they don't necessarily see the life-changing potential you have to offer.

So, how do we help others?

The permission slip of awareness I had, when I left my marriage, was my kids. This may sound backwards to many, as most believe you should stay in a marriage even when you don't want to be there, for the sake of the kids. My realization was that if my kids were in a similar situation as myself, what would I want them to do? The answer of course, is to follow their own guidance and do what is best for them, which would be to leave. How could I expect my kids to do this, if I didn't lead by example?

Being a living example is the best way to help others. Make your life a priority by living it in the best possible leading edge way you know how, which will then inspire those who are ready to ask you how to do it. Before long you'll have people asking you why your life is filled with magic. Why life is so easy for you. How you achieve so much with so little effort. When they open up to these questions, they are now in the receiving mode for the lessons you have to offer.

If you don't feel like teaching them, that's okay, too. Helping others is not your responsibility – they have an inner being for that. You could always just hand them a copy of this book.

So, how do we truly break free from the rules and bounds society imposes upon us? The simple answer is to keep the knowingness at the forefront by affirming, "I came here to live life for me." Nobody knows what's best for you. The only person who truly knows is your inner being. Parents, friends, co-workers may think they know, but in reality, they have no idea.

HONOR YOU

> **Give yourself full permission to be fully you. Remind yourself that everyone else's perceptions and judgements come from their own programming, their own path, and their own life experiences which are fully irrelevant to you.**

If you struggle with your authenticity, work through your own negative self-criticisms, judgments and fears around being that person. Remember, the authentic you is the person you came here to be.

HONOR YOUR EXCITEMENT

Does training to climb the world's tallest mountain excite you? Do that. Does being in a polyamorous relationship excite you? Do that. Does working as a psychic medium excite you? Do that. Do you want to live alone in a boat off the coast of Costa Rica? Do that. Does the idea of developing the world's tastiest cheese excite you? Do that.

Excitement isn't something you have to rationalize. As previously mentioned, it's guidance from your inner being. The things that excite you do so because they are part of your path. Some things that excite, like ordering pizza from your favorite pizza joint or becoming a nurse, may fit into the norms of society. Others, like being in a polyamorous relationship or working as a psychic medium, may not. This doesn't invalidate these experiences or your excitement for them. Just because they don't fit into the same excitements and you could be judged by others, doesn't make them bad or wrong.

> **When we ignore our authenticity and what we truly desire, we are not honoring who we really are and our path.**

YOU'RE NOT ALONE

Sometimes it can get lonely on the leading edge. It's not uncommon to feel misunderstood or abandoned by those around us. Sometimes typical mainstream conversations around topics such as politics, sports, or who's paying the most on their power bill no longer feel fulfilling and it's hard to connect with others.

As we expand and grow in awareness, so do our desires, and the things that excite us may change and no longer match up with those who are familiar in our lives. That's okay, and you're not alone. Be open and allowing to new people showing up.

The friends I had before 2012 may be long gone, but new ones who are much more aligned to who I am have shown up. Anik and I have attended conferences all around the world and our best friends and those we connect with the most are spread all around the planet, from California to the United Kingdom to the tiny island of Mallorca.

Our friends may be spread out around the globe, but yours don't need to be. Remember, you're the creator of your reality and you have the power to manifest friends who are aligned with who you truly are, right in your own backyard.

MEET YOU 2.0

In the context of manifestation, most people set their sights on manifesting things like money, relationships, and health. But have you ever taken a step back to work on manifesting the self you truly desire to be?

No, I'm not asking you to attempt to clone yourself (although that could be very handy if you could pull it off). I'm talking about the version of you that has the desires and has achieved the things you've been looking to achieve when you first picked up this book.

In the very first session with many of my clients, I give them a piece of homework called the YOU 2.0.

Who, or what, is YOU 2.0?

You 2.0 is the next version, or iteration, of you. It's who you are on your way to becoming, or who you desire to become. It's the version of you that has already manifested the desires and is living your dream life. The version of you who has the freedom, relationship, wealth, and health you seek.

Getting the clarity on your 2.0 is an important exercise, as this is who you want to embody and become so that the reality you desire then transforms to match that person's vibrational frequency. Remember, you need to become this person first, so reality will transform to reflect it.

With pen and a paper, jump to a point in time in the future where you have become this person. A point in time where you have all the desires you seek. Where you are living the life you want to step into.

Speaking in present tense, write about what you see. Write about your future surroundings, where your 2.0 lives, what your life looks like. How you earn an income. Describe You 2.0's relationship. Most importantly, describe how you feel. Do you feel successful? Confident? Good Enough? How does your day look? How does that version of you think? What actions do you take? Speak about all of this, as detailed as you can, in present tense.

Once you've completed this exercise, your next goal is to be that person now. Create a mental imprint of that version of you and embody it. Act as they would act. Practice the confidence and feeling of success they feel. Merge that 2.0 you down into who you really are. This will help you practice the vibration of where and who you want to be, drawing it closer into your physical reality.

When doing this exercise, it may bring up fears or make other elements of resistance apparent. You may be afraid to speak up in the way your 2.0 speaks up. You may be afraid to embrace your next iterations sense of confidence or self worth. That's okay. Identifying these pockets of resistance is part of the process. Identifying and dealing with these using the clearing process taught earlier in this book will ultimately help bridge the gap to where you want to be.

THE MANIFESTATION GODS ARE WATCHING

One of the biggest secrets to all this work, maybe even the biggest secret of all, is the importance of the intent behind the work itself.

I'm unable to explain exactly why, or how, but in my experience, when you are seeking out manifestations or to live in the new paradigm, there is one very important rule.

Don't do the work for the sake of achieving an outcome.

It's almost as if the manifestation gods are watching down upon us and are aware of the intent behind what we do.

If you're doing these practices or exercises from the intent of doing them to make something happen, this displeases the gods and it seems to slow down the manifestation process.

If you're doing the work and these processes with the sole intent to feel good; with the sole intent of how much joy and satisfaction can I experience today; if you do your embodiment work and embody desires for the joy of the daydream rather than doing them to "make it showup;" you are pleasing the manifestation gods, accelerating manifestation.

Of course, there is no such thing as the manifestation gods, but that brings up another important point.

> ## Are you hoping for your desires to show up, or are you choosing them?

When I look at the law of attraction landscape, most men and women are in the state of hoping. Praying that the universe, source, God, or their inner being will reward them for being in alignment and deliver to them what they want.

If this sounds like you, what you may be forgetting, is that universe, source, God, your inner being, is you. It's all you. It's the nonphysical part of you.

Why is this important?

Imagine you see a pencil on your desk that you'd like to pick up. Do you hope to pick it up, or do you choose to pick it up? You choose to pick it up, so you walk over and do it.

In physical reality, you can choose because you know that you can use your arms and hands to pick that pencil up. You consciously understand that you have the ability and control to make that happen. You choose it, and it happens.

In the context of manifestation, hope contains the energy of doubt but as you know, manifestation comes with high levels of certainty. Just because you can't rationally see how the manifestation of a desire will unfold in the same way picking up a pencil unfolds, doesn't make it any less certain. All of physical reality is an extension of the nonphysical you, and the nonphysical you can deliver anything, just in the same way you can pick up the pencil.

So, don't hope for it. Choose it. Set your sights on your desire and proclaim that it is yours, that it is already done.

Practice with conviction and certainty that it is yours, and from a place free of doubt, it will be.

CHAPTER KEY CONCEPT SUMMARY

- Instead of chasing after specific manifestations, embrace seeking out the new paradigm as a priority, relying on the mechanism of synchronicity to do the work.

- The self-help journey is a journey of undoing, of returning to our authenticity and who we really are, as well as uncovering our true power as creators.

- The perceptions of society and how it states we should be living our lives is often the greatest barrier to embracing the new paradigm and living on the leading edge.

- By not honoring your excitement and holding back in favor of keeping other people pleased, you are preventing yourself from moving down your path and what you came here to experience.

- Your path may be different than what others believe you should be doing, and they may not understand it. It's not your job to make them understand. Acknowledge that they aren't you and they can never know what is truly best for you. Only your inner being knows.

- There is nothing wrong with choosing to live within the norms of society; we all have the freedom to choose how we want to live our lives. For some, our path is to experience the leading edge, and for others, it's not. It isn't your job to convince someone to follow the same path as you.

- If you want to help others, be the example by living your truth, which then gives others a permission slip to do the same.

- You came here to live life for nobody else but you.

- Honor yourself and your excitement – you are exactly who you came here to be.

- You are not alone.

- Do the work and exercises not from the vantage point of achieving an outcome, but from the vantage point of how good these exercises will make you feel.

- Practice the energy of choosing your desires rather than hoping for them.

EPILOGUE: WELCOME TO THE NEW PARADIGM – FINAL THOUGHTS

Welcome to the new paradigm.

Welcome to the understanding, and the awareness, that your life is a projection, not of who you are, but who you believe you are. A projection of how you've chosen to see the world and how you've chosen to see yourself.

You have been given what I believe is everything you could ever need to truly step into your power. To truly embody and allow the unfolding of the life experience desired when you first chose to experience this physical reality. To master the art of Power Manifesting.

WHAT HAPPENS NEXT IS UP TO YOU

I want you to ask yourself two very simple yet important questions.

First, how long have you been studying the Law of Attraction or concepts similar to these? Has it been weeks, months, years, or longer?

Second, think about that one thing you really want. Is it a relationship? Money? Perfect health? In what way were

237

you hoping this book would change your life when you first picked it up? Have you been seeking freedom? Inner peace? Satisfaction? Or, maybe that ease, flow and luxuriously abundant lifestyle you've always felt deep down is available to you?

That one thing you've been chasing, that one thing you really want, how long have you been after it? Years? Decades? Maybe your entire life?

As I've traveled all over the world to seminars by some of the world's top self-help and spiritual teachers, I've met men and women who have been chasing their desires, some for well over a decade, and yet continue to struggle to live that life of ease and let in the big things they really want.

I don't want you to be one of those people.

I don't want it to take you the greater part of a decade to live the life you really want. I don't want you to spend the greater part of your physical reality experience endlessly chasing after something that constantly sits just at the tip of your nose. I don't want you to be one of those people who keeps running into the same brick wall after brick wall, feeling stuck, disempowered, and hopeless.

I know what's possible for you, and now, hopefully, you see it too. For many of those who struggle, it's not because they don't want it. It's not because they don't deserve the abundance. It's not because they don't understand the concepts. It's simply because they don't commit to applying them.

What's the difference between an amateur craftsman and a professional who creates amazing pieces? Over time professionals, through their dedication, have refined their skills, they've applied what they've learned, and have committed to their practice. They worked with other masters who've learned from their own life experiences and who've shown them the way.

If you came to this book simply looking for a better understanding of the principles taught in this book, the journey ends here, and I hope you enjoyed reading it.

But, if you came here looking for change, looking for the key to real transformation – bigger manifestations and more of what you want – your journey is likely just beginning, and that is truly an exciting place to be.

Remember this.

There is no such thing as lack. Only the experience of lack and everything you desire is truly available to you.

You are a powerful creator – we all are. Far more powerful than we can ever imagine, and as you walk down this path, you will discover more of how powerful you truly are.

You are good enough. You are exactly who you came here to be. Everything about you was molded in perfection from the nonphysical. Judgments of other people or of your inner critic have no bearing on how amazing you truly are. You are without a doubt good enough to be, do or have, anything you truly want.

I believe in you. You've got this. No matter how many times I've worked with clients who said this or that seems impossible, it's never been the case. I know that you, just like anyone else, can accomplish anything, and the teachings from this book, if applied, will guide you there.

You are supported. You are supported by me. By your inner being. By those around you even if they don't express it or seem like they don't care. Everything you need to walk your path and achieve your desires is always being provided to you from the nonphysical. If you ever feel lost or alone, you're welcome to reach out via my website, my social media channels, or to join the collective, my online community.

You are never stuck. A circumstance is nothing more than a vibration you keep practicing. If you feel stuck, you're simply practicing a specific vibration over and over again. Every minute, every millisecond, is a brand-new moment offering a brand-new opportunity to practice a new vibration. All vibrations are always available to everyone, and by that understanding alone, you are never stuck.

Enjoy the journey. The unfolding will never end. The further you allow your way down your path, the better things get and the more there is to discover. You'll never get it done, so take your journey one day at a time, one step at a time. Find the joy in the process, and the process will serve you beyond your wildest dreams.

WHERE TO GO FROM HERE

I don't want to just give you a book and send you on your way. I'm passionate about seeing real people experience real change, and that extends to my readers.

In my experience, one of the keys to success is surrounding yourself with a community of like-minded people who share the same vision and goals for success that you do. I attribute a large part of my personal success to attending conferences and connecting with the right people all over the world, people who had achieved the things I wanted, or who were on the path to getting there. I suggest sharing this book with friends who may be on a similar journey and recommend working through the exercises presented in this book together. A strong support structure has been invaluable to me, and I'm sure would be to you as well.

If you're serious about taking the knowledge shared in this book and applying it, I highly recommend checking out the Power Manifesting Collective. This is my online community focused on guiding members through these teachings and applying the concepts in this book. You can find information about the collective at http://nickbreau.com/trialthecollective/.

I APPRECIATE YOUR APPRECIATION

Thank you for reading this book. Thank you for being you and shining your light in this world. Thank you for embarking on this path of self exploration. It is not your responsibility to help others, but your commitment to yourself creates a positive ripple effect to everyone around you.

If you enjoyed this book and feel drawn to sharing your appreciation, I would love to hear what you enjoyed the most about this book. Feel free to drop a review on Amazon or visit http://nickbreau.com/appreciate.

A PARTING GIFT FROM ME TO YOU

If I were to ask you for your favorite part of attending a birthday party when you were a child, what would you answer? Was it the games you would play? The time you'd spend with friends? Getting to eat cake?

When my kids were younger, what excited them the most was the goodies bag. A little bag of surprise treats waiting for them as a parting gift once the party was over. The excitement on their faces when they'd open up the bag to see what was inside will be hard to forget.

Although reading a book isn't quite the same as a childhood birthday party (what's a party without cake?), I've decided to throw in a bit of party magic by putting together a goodbye goodies bag just for you! You can claim your goodies by visiting http://nickbreau.com/goodies.

APPENDIX

THE POWER MANIFESTING PROTOCOL

In this section, we put it all together. I've taken everything we've explored in this book and we put it into a practical, step-by-step general reference so that you allow your way into the new paradigm of how to experience physical reality.

If you're just picking up the book for the first time, saw the title of the chapter, and skipped right to this point, I urge you to go back. Taking the time to understand each element in the protocol will help reinforce its importance and make sure you're doing it from the right energy.

You can use this as a checklist or reference to keep you in check. If at any point along your life journey you feel stuck or struggling, you can come back to this chapter to trouble-shoot what you may, or may not be doing that you should or shouldn't be.

1. Focus on feeling good.

    As previously explained, you can't fool the gods of the Law of Attraction. Make sure you are doing the work for no other reason than to feel good. This should be your primary life priority. How much fun, joy, and satisfaction can I feel? How much fun can I integrate in everything that I do? If you are trying to use the Law of Attraction to work your way out of a problem or manifest something specific, you may be keeping yourself stuck there with a current reality loop.

Remember, the law of attraction isn't about manipulating reality so that you can manifest what you need to feel better. It's about feeling better, so that physical reality then molds to your new vibrational good feeling place.

How can you tell if you're doing this right?

Are you applying this work from the context of:

a) Manifesting a specific desire
b) Working your way out of a problem or unwanted circumstance
c) Feeling good

If your answer is c) then you're taking the right approach. This doesn't mean that a) and b) won't happen. It's about understanding that c) is the path of least resistance for achieving (or should I say allowing) both a) and b).

2. Reach for alignment.

Are you busy trying to make things happen through effort and action, or are you reaching for feeling good and alignment so you can better make use of the mechanism of synchronicity? How do you know you are in alignment? The only true measure is how good you feel. If you question whether you are or aren't in alignment, you likely aren't in it.

3. If you struggle with alignment or feeling good.

When alignment is a challenge or a struggle, take the following action steps.

a) Implement and commit to a solid morning practice, play the F-It Happy game.

b) If you are dominantly in struggle, reach for relief. If in relief, reach for satisfaction, and if in satisfaction, reach for turned on and then bliss.

c) Identify and clear the dominant negative emotions preventing alignment or making it a challenge.

d) Use the negative emotions as the guidance system they are, and work through the perspectives that trigger negative emotions.

e) Don't be hard on yourself. Not everyone achieves high alignment all the time – it's a practice and skill you will develop over time.

4. Follow your excitement.

Excitement is your highest form of intuition and guidance from your inner being. Your course of action in any moment is to follow your path of highest excitement without doubt or question. Ask yourself "In this moment, what excites me the most?" Honor your excitement and your flow. Remember that the next step along your path of excitement doesn't need to be grandiose – it could be as simple as taking a nap.

5. Get clear on your desires.

In order to move forward along your path and continue to create positive momentum, make sure you get clear and focused on your desires and embody them. Write them down in present tense and uses processes such as the Into Existence process (also included in the appendix).

6. Get clear on your 2.0.

   Are you clear on who you are or who you want to be? Just as you would for your desires, get clear on who the future version of you is who has achieved what you would currently like to achieve. How does this version of you think, feel and act? Embody this version of you as much as you can in your current reality.

7. Don't push against contrast.

   You'll never escape contrast, it's an ongoing part of the human experience and necessary for your evolution and expansion. You can, however, move more quickly through it. When contrast presents itself to you, don't push against it, and, rather than jumping into emergency fix-it mode, self-reflect and take action from a vibrational standpoint.

   If people or circumstances are creating a yoyo effect with your emotions, remember that your work isn't to change those people or those circumstances. Your work is to identify and work with the emotions and perspectives they trigger in you, so they no longer create a triggering effect that pulls you down. In doing so, these circumstances will also change.

8. Be vibrationally productive.

   Be mindful of not getting caught up in action and effort to accomplish your goals rather than vibrational action-taking. How much of your day is spent and focused on feeling good rather than on efforting to accomplish? Are you taking action out of effort as a means to accomplish, or are you taking action out of inspiration, detached from the outcome?

9. Act out of the energy of fun.

   Stress and pressure to accomplish and achieve something are manifestation blockers. Joy and fun are manifestation fuel that bring things into existence. When approaching a task, doing so from the vantage point of "How much fun or joy can I experience doing this?" rather than from the energy of the need to get something done just to get it done, will yield very different results.

10. Dream and get out ahead of it.

    How much time are you spending focused on current reality circumstances versus dreaming about where you truly want to be? Remember that where you put your focus is where you're setting your sails to. Ensure that when you focus on where you want to be, it also feels good and exciting; otherwise you may be creating momentum in the wrong direction.

Each of these points may take you several weeks or even months to become proficient. Remember, the process is the point. The more you're okay with where you're at, the more you enjoy the unfolding and the practice of mastery of these concepts, the quicker you will find yourself evolving to new levels of manifestation.

THE POWER MANIFESTING INTO EXISTENCE PROCESS

In the summer of 2019, I created a process named the Into Existence Process, which I share with my one on one clients and The Power Manifesting Collective, my group membership community. This process is designed to help you fully embody specific desires in every way possible, to help you become a vibrational match to them.

Your dominant intent in this process is to indulge in the positive-feeling state of these specific exercises. Perform them for the pleasure of the dream and the feeling state these exercises provide for you, and not from the energy of trying to make something happen.

In this process, you will be performing specific embodiment exercises for one desire you'd like to manifest. Each day you will practice a different form of embodiment, for four days, and then on the fifth day, practice getting in the receiving mode. This process only ever needs to be done once.

Day 1. Write it into existence

Get clear, get specific, get detailed about your desire. Put a pen on paper and WRITE.

How does it look, feel, smell, taste, and touch?

What emotions do you feel, what does the experience of it look and feel like?

Get as detailed as you possibly can in order to build as much momentum as possible.

Day 2. Speak it into existence [3-5 TIMES TODAY]

Talk about the desire out loud. Record it on your phone or use a timer (no need to listen, you can delete it right away). How much can you say about your desire in two to five minutes? Rampage it out. Use your notes from Day 1 if you struggle with this.

Day 3. Embody it into existence (audio)

Use my Embodiment Meditation. This meditation is available for free in the bonus companion resources at http://nickbreau.com/bonus.

Day 4. Live it into existence (from the energy ready to be ready)

Today, spend your day embodying that desire to its fullest as if it already exists.

Are you looking to manifest a Porsche? Do everything from the energy of being a Porsche owner. This is how it feels to make coffee as a Porsche owner. This is how it feels to gas my car up as a Porsche owner. This is how it feels to play hockey as a Porsche owner.

Day 5. Receiving mode day (relief+satisfaction)

Get into the receiving mode. Stay completely off the topic of your desire; don't think about it, don't notice its absence, don't work your way into it or try and figure anything out. Today, your only commitment is to determine how much satisfaction, fun, and happiness you can feel.

THE POWER MANIFESTING MORNING PRACTICE

The goal of your morning practice is to achieve the best feeling place possible. Feel as good as you can, as early as possible in the day (before negative self talk has had a chance to set in), then practice holding that positive emotional place (the F-It Happy game).

Different practices work for different people. For some, twenty minutes of yoga may be uplifting and energizing. For others, it could be listening to country music or doing origami. There are no rules to the morning practice, other than the activities you commit to should be things you know uplift and make you feel good. If your morning practice feels too much like effort, be cautious, as it may be doing more harm than good.

Start small, one or two activities perhaps, and work your way up if possible. We all have different morning commitments as well. A single mom with five kids may have less time to commit to a practice than someone who works from home with flexible hours. Those with little time may do some of these exercises before getting out of bed, while in the shower or even during their commute.

The following practice is the template I share with most clients. Remember, this is only a guideline, and you'll want to try some of these activities, keeping those you like and throwing out the rest.

Start with the Morning Rampage audio (available in the bonus companion resources at http://nickbreau.com/bonus). Finish with my guided Positive Momentum Meditation audio (also available in the bonus companion resources). Activities I suggest between those two audios:

- Appreciation Journaling

- Movement (yoga, tai chi, paddleboard, go for a walk)

- Listen to uplifting audio (upbeat music, Abraham-Hicks recordings)

- Fresh juice, satisfying smoothie or delicious coffee. Indulge in what you eat.

- Silent or other forms of meditation

- Positive Aspect lists (write down statements that bring up the feelings of ease, relief, satisfaction, freedom, joy, etc.)

When it comes to implementing a morning practice, it may feel like effort for the first few weeks until a routine develops. That's okay – give it a bit of time and stick with it for at least two to three weeks. I've had a number of men and women share with me that doing this practice for just four weeks completely changed their life.

KEY PROBING AND ATTRACTION POINT AUDIT STATEMENTS

The following is a listing of the key probing statements I've shared with you in this book. Here they serve as a reference for working through your negative emotions by identifying the underlying perspectives.

NEGATIVE EMOTION PROBING STATEMENTS

1. What must I believe to be true in order to feel this way?
2. I feel this way because ...

Example:
Emotion: Not Good Enough:
Question: What must I believe is true to feel not good enough?
Answer: Nobody invited me to the dance this weekend.
Next Step: Reframe the answer to shift your perspective, then probe again if necessary.

FEAR AND ANXIETY PROBING STATEMENTS

1. This feel unsafe because ...
2. If I choose to do this one thing that feels unsafe, what's the worst thing that could happen?

Example:
Fear: It's not safe to publish my book.
Question: This feels unsafe because ...
Answer: People might judge me.
Next Step: Reframe or probe deeper (i.e. That feels unsafe because ...)

AUDITING YOUR ATTRACTION POINT

Use the following circumstances to identify if you have any dominant negative emotions impacting your attraction point. If the same emotions keep surfacing over and over again, this is indicative of a dominant negative emotion you'll want to work through.

For each of these circumstances, write down the 1-3 negative emotions triggered when you ask the question **What is the worst part of this circumstance and how does this circumstance make me feel?**

- The one thing in life that stresses me out the most or creates the most pressure.

- Your financial situation.

- Your current relationship (or lack of).

- Past significant romantic relationships.

- Your career or current job (or lack of).

- Family members you may butt heads against or who trigger you.

- Health conditions or weight issues.

- Significant past traumas or circumstances with strong emotional charge.

Example:

- The one thing in life that stresses me out the most or creates the most pressure.

  I can't find someone to buy my house, it's been over a year, this makes me feel stuck and powerless.

- Your financial situation.

  I can barely pay my bills and can't find another source of income. I feel stuck and not good enough.

- Your current relationship (or lack of).

  I can never please my partner – no matter what I do, it's never good enough and it makes me angry.

- Past significant romantic relationships.

  Relationship 1: They cheated on me twice; this made me feel stuck and not good enough.

  Relationship 2: They were controlling; I couldn't do what I wanted; this made me feel stuck.

  Relationship 3: They would never listen to what I had to say; this made me feel stuck.

- Your career or current job (or lack of).

  My boss is micromanaging and never leaves me alone. He's never pleased. This makes me feel stuck, frustrated and not good enough.

- Family members you may butt heads against or who trigger you.

  My dad is always judging and criticizing what I do; it makes me feel not good enough.

- Health conditions or weight issues.

I struggle to lose weight; no matter what I do I never see results. This makes me feel angry and stuck.

- Significant past traumas or circumstances with a strong emotional charge.

  I was the victim of financial fraud last year; this made me feel like a victim and stuck.

Results: In this example, this person has strong dominant negative emotions of not good enough and feeling stuck. These are the emotions they should work through in order to more easily achieve alignment and to stop attracting circumstances that reflect these emotions in their current reality.

ABOUT THE AUTHOR

Nick Breau is an international Breakthrough Specialist and Law of Attraction expert who over the last decade has served clients in over twenty five countries.

Labeled computer hacker turned people hacker, Nick started his career in tech where he played in a variety of startup companies. After nearly a decade of analyzing, troubleshooting and solving complex problems in software systems, his career led him to playing a key role in a $330 million acquisition. He then walked away from the tech world to focus on what inspires him most, helping people.

Nick has now spent over a decade studying self-help and personal development including topics such as the subconscious mind, human behavior, the nature of reality, the Law of Attraction, mental and emotional healing, what drives success and what keeps people stuck. His private clients have ranged from CEOs, Wallstreet traders, FBI agents and lawyers to teachers, musicians, members of the entertainment industry and even stay-at-home moms.

Nick's greatest passion is exploring the power of the mind and pushing the leading edge of what's possible in physical reality. He lives in a small town on the Atlantic coast of Canada with his partner Anik where he runs an online community called The Power Manifesting Collective.

For more on Nick's work visit http://nickbreau.com